IMAGES
of America

CROWN HEIGHTS
AND WEEKSVILLE

IMAGES
of America

CROWN HEIGHTS
AND WEEKSVILLE

Wilhelmena Rhodes Kelly

ARCADIA
PUBLISHING

Published by Arcadia Publishing
Charleston SC, Chicago IL, Portsmouth NH, San Francisco CA

Library of Congress Control Number: 2009922408

For all general information contact Arcadia Publishing at:
Telephone 843-853-2070
Fax 843-853-0044
E-mail sales@arcadiapublishing.com
For customer service and orders:
Toll-Free 1-888-313-2665

Visit us on the Internet at www.arcadiapublishing.com

CONTENTS

Acknowledgments   6

Introduction   7

1.   Early History   9

2.   Institutions and Services   25

3.   People and Places   55

4.   Rest and Relaxation   81

5.   Accidents and Incidents   99

6.   Architectural Gems   115

Bibliography   127

ACKNOWLEDGMENTS

Special thanks go to Brian Merlis of Brooklynpix.com, whose ongoing commitment to Brooklyn history and its preservation provided a depth and variety of images without which this book would not have been possible. I also appreciate the support and cooperation of Barbara Killens-Rivera, Ahmed Smith Ford, Linda Jones, Anthony Wilkins, Dorothy Hamlin Rhodes, Janet Ross, Paula Hamlin Murphy and Gregory Hamlin, Dolores McCullough, Miriam Lowenstein, Rabbi Isroel Gordon, Devorah Rosenfeld, Brooklyn College Special Collections, Joy Holland and June Kuffi of Brooklyn Public Library Brooklyn Collections, Weeksville Heritage Center, Patrick McNamara and the Brooklyn Archdiocese, Martha Millard, the David Library of the American Revolution at Washington's Crossing in Pennsylvania, my editor Erin Vosgien and proofreader Heather Fernald at Arcadia Publishing, and the Crown Heights North Association with Deborah Young and Suzanne Spellen.

Anyone interested in the preservation of history, architectural beauty, and neighborhood integrity may contact me at mena23219@msn.com. Your suggestions, ideas, and stories of past successes will be welcomed.

All uncredited photographs were provided by the author.

INTRODUCTION

The neighborhood of Crown Heights, and the smaller microcommunity of Weeksville contained within it, are today part of the densely populated metropolis of Brooklyn, New York. Housing more then 300,000 residents in its four-square-mile boundaries, or over 10 percent of the borough's population of two and a half million, the history of the founding, development, and expansion of this urban location has been largely influenced by a single factor: its once formidable and challenging topography.

Ensconced in some of the highest elevations in New York City, the Crown Heights that one sees today has been shaped by the huge terminal moraine that is its base. Even from its earliest founding, this rough and primeval foundation arrested the early economic growth and agricultural worth of its budding hamlets.

Bordering on Peter Stuyvesant's 1660s acquisition of 395 acres from the Lenape Indians, Crown Heights remained a dense and heavily wooded location held as common property by local residents. In fact, years later, the British would need a scout to lead them through the dense brush during the Battle of Long Island in August 1776.

From the earliest years, the flat and fertile terrain of the townships of Bedford to the north and Flatbush to the south grew abundant produce, which enriched both towns significantly. Meanwhile the rock-ridden precipice that was the future spine of Crown Heights remained a wilderness.

These common woods, largely unsuited for farming, were consequently parceled out over the years, with the wooded hills becoming home to squatters. Even as the construction of neighborhood housing grew, it was not until the 1850s that institutions serving the sick, orphaned, imprisoned, and poor would realize the affordability of the hilly outpost.

Weeksville, an independent black community founded shortly after New York's 1827 emancipation of its enslaved population, established a presence in the 1830s and prospered over time in the area's remote environs. The land was initially purchased by Henry C. Thompson from the Leffert Lefferts estate in the 1830s.

In 1838, James Weeks, an African American freedman from North Carolina who worked as a stevedore on the New York docks, purchased land from Thompson. Weeks soon made his home near the location of Atlantic and Buffalo Avenues, which became the center of Weeksville, a black township comprised primarily of local freedmen and transplanted African Americans with a population of more than 500 residents by the 1850s.

In time, the hamlet grew, creating its own colored school, Citizens Union Cemetery, *Torchlight* newspaper, African Civilization Society, Howard Colored Orphanage, and Methodist, Episcopal, and Baptist churches. Bethel Tabernacle Church, founded in 1847 and still an icon in the neighborhood, is recognized as the first church in Weeksville. The historic Berean Missionary Baptist Church, also a local religious institution, dates back to that early era as well with its 1850 founding. St. Phillips Episcopal Church too (with its edifice on McDonough Street in nearby Bedford-Stuyvesant) had its beginnings in the early town.

Growth in Weeksville continued steadily, with a large jump in population realized at the outbreak of the Manhattan Civil War draft riots in July 1863. The burning of the New York Colored Orphanage at Forty-second Street and Fifth Avenue, random lynchings, and aggressive home invasions forced many blacks to seek refuge in Brooklyn.

Eventually the glacial moraine, created approximately 17,000 years ago by the receding Wisconsin glacier, was tamed by leveling the mountains and filling the hollows. Construction of local roadways soon followed, along with improved transportation, increased moderate frame housing, fine brownstone properties, and the ultimate destruction of a once rural lifestyle.

In time, the smaller townships of Carsville and Pigtown also emerged as separate identifiable communities, with many named after the communities' local hills, such as Ocean Hill, Crow Hill, and Prospect Hill (becoming Prospect Heights), or as in the case of Brownsville and Malboneville, after local founders.

The Catholic Church also exerted a large influence on the settlement of what would become the Crown Heights neighborhood. A growing parish in the late 1800s brought about the founding and construction of not only magnificent local churches but also church elementary schools, high schools, a college, hospitals, and orphanages.

These included the churches of St. Matthew, St. Ignatius, St. Gregory the Great, and nearby St. Teresa, as well as the Brooklyn Preparatory School and College, St. Mary's Hospital, St. Joseph's School for the Deaf, St. John's Home for Boys, the Bishop McDonnell Catholic High School for Girls, and the nearby Bishop Loughlin High School for Boys.

Advances in easy accessibility to expanded surface and later local subway transportation, along with the 1883 completion of the Brooklyn Bridge and Brooklyn's ultimate 1888 merger with Manhattan, also brought change to the neighborhood. The early 20th century saw Crown Heights evolve into a melting pot of races, religions, and cultures from Irish, German, Italian, African American, Caribbean, Protestant, Jewish, and Catholic backgrounds.

That evolution continues today, and with those ongoing changes, clear evidence of the early, rural foundations of Crown Heights and Weeksville is also disappearing. It is only the challenging hill, rare 19th-century frame house, fragment of cobblestoned road peering through asphalt, or unexplained alley ending abruptly that now hint at the neighborhood's past.

This is a look at that past and does not pretend to be a deep, comprehensive history. It is simply an effort to provide an overview of what came before, and in doing so, recognize the lives that were lived and the life stories that were played out, often anonymously. In remembering the local residents who once struggled with the challenges of life in the evolving communities of central Brooklyn, it also helps document some of those early struggles for those descendant Americans—now living in all corners of the country—whose lives were shaped by those efforts.

One

EARLY HISTORY

The neighborhood of Crown Heights was at one time a deeply wooded, sparsely populated location perched atop soaring hills once known to locals as the Green Mountains. These formidable peaks are in fact a terminal moraine made of the stony debris of rocks, soil, and boulders from the Wisconsin glacier's final retreat 17,000 years ago.

Crown Heights was the former home of western Long Island's native Lenape Indians. It borders on the land acquired by the Dutch in a 1662 grant approved by New Amsterdam governor Pieter Stuyvesant and the Dutch East Indian Company. Local residents Jan Joris Rapalje, Teunis Gysbert Bogaert, Cornelius Jacobsen, Hendrick Sweers, Michael Hans (Bergen), and Jan Hans (Bergen) each acquired "20-morgen" (40 acres) of land for cultivation in the northern township later to become Bedford.

These men were the first of many to invest in this Central Brooklyn location, with Leffert Pieterse of Flatbush Township making a purchase in 1700. From its Bedford location, with the Lefferts family among the area's wealthiest and most influential landholders, local investors continued to expand their acquisition of vast acreage, which included the formidable hills within Crown Heights.

The earliest settlers called this tract the Common Lands, and in the April 16, 1739, Kings County Register of Conveyances (Liber 5, page 94) parcels of narrow 10-acre strips, one to each named settler, provided fuel and grazing for his cattle. These parallel strips ran from Degraw Street (now Lincoln Place) and extended southeasterly to the old "Patent Line," the Flatbush border.

Over time, given its remote nature, the townships of Weeksville and Carsville also found its affordable location ideal. Generations of squatters would inhabit these wooded hills creating legal obstacles that later hindered development of the area.

It was the push to construct the Eastern Parkway in 1870, however, that ultimately uprooted the area, and in doing so forced it to keep pace with Brooklyn's burgeoning development.

This 12-mile bird's-eye view of 1842 New York shows the juxtaposition of Manhattan, Brooklyn, Staten Island, and New Jersey. Major roads appear as mere tracery, including the dotted line that traverses from east to west through Brooklyn, here labeled "Long Island." (New York Public Library, Map Division.)

The terminal moraine, home of today's Crown Heights, creates a formidable barrier between Bedford to the north and Flatbush Township to the south. Numbers mark the locations of major pathways used during the Revolutionary War skirmishes: No. 2, the Flatbush Pass; No. 3, Clove Road (also known as Bedford Pass); and No. 4, Jamaica Pass. (The David Library of the American Revolution.)

America's Gen. John Sullivan fought the British in the Battle of Long Island in August 1776. Sullivan Place, a street in Crown Heights, is named for the Maine-born Patriot and war hero. Ebbets Field was once located on Sullivan Place and Bedford Avenue, now the intersection of the Ebbets Field Apartments.

Hessian foot soldiers pitched camp at the Crown Heights intersection of Franklin Avenue and Bergen Street during the seven-year British occupation of New York from 1776 to 1783. This 1930s photograph is of the exact location of those camps. Until the ground was leveled in 1852, the position of the flagstaff and entrance of the camp was still visible. (New York Public Library.)

A snapshot of that street today shows very little has changed during the course of the past 70 years. The corner building still stands, although now unoccupied. The block, zoned for industrial occupation, once produced beer and canned foods. The Heinz Company operated a factory in that block, and its corporate name is still faintly visible at the top of the far left building.

VIEW ON LOWER SIDE.

Hessian and British Revolutionary War solders lived in quarters such as these during their seven–year occupation of Manhattan and Brooklyn's Bedford township. The redoubt was built into the earth, created by digging a trench 30 to 50 feet long and about 12 or 15 feet wide. British officers, however, commandeered local homes for their own personal residences, including the homes of the local Lefferts family.

SECTIONAL VIEW.

This sectional view illustrates the interior construction of this redoubt. A board resting on the excavated bank formed a roof, and each hut had a large stone fireplace or two for warmth as needed. Over the years, many relics have been found in this former camping ground, and human skeletons were often discovered during the grading of the hilly land.

Located on Pacific Street near Kingston Avenue, this 1850s frame structure is the oldest house in Crown Heights. It once looked out on open planting fields and is now densely surrounded by multiple-family, three- and four-story dwellings. (New York City Municipal Archives.)

The intersection of Bedford Avenue at Ulysses S. Grant Square, once featured a fountain (right) at this Crown Heights and Bedford-Stuyvesant juncture near Atlantic Avenue. At that time, the Unity Club still retained its distinctive steeple, and the women (barely discernable) walking past the building were still wearing long skirts and modest dark colors. (Brooklyn Public Library Brooklyn Collection.)

Pigtown at Troy Avenue and Montgomery Street is an example of the rural and rough housing that existed as late as the 1920s. At right is the Peck Memorial Hospital, in the process of being constructed in 1918. Once a predominantly Italian neighborhood in the early 20th century, the area was noted for its free-roaming livestock, including the occasional goat spotted along the roadways. (Brian Merlis.)

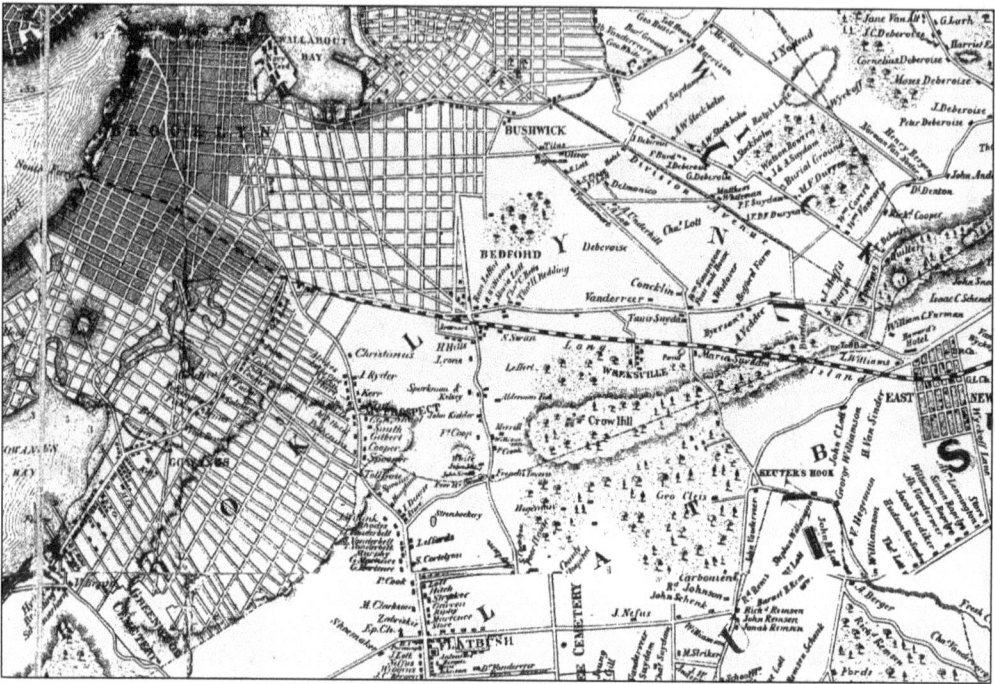

Grids of densely developed city blocks are held at bay by the hills of Crown Heights. The Crow Hill peak and the Weeksville community to the north are clearly labeled in this segment of an 1842 map. (New York Public Library, Map Division.)

The African American community of Weeksville was founded in the early 1830s, shortly after New York eliminated slavery in the state in 1827. The large landholding family of Leffert Lefferts sold the initial acreage to Henry C. Thompson, who in turn sold property to James Weeks, for whom the village was eventually named. (Brian Merlis.)

The Bethel Tabernacle African Methodist Episcopal (AME) Church was organized in 1847 at the corner of Schenectady Avenue and Dean Street and continues to be a religious presence in the Weeksville community today. In 1978, the congregation purchased and then moved across the street into the former PS 83 building at Bergen Street and Schenectady, where it still resides. (Weeksville Heritage Center.)

The Reverend Edward C. Africanus (1821–1853) was the first pastor of the Bethel Tabernacle AME Church in Weeksville, and from 1850 to 1853, he was pastor of the Macedonia AME Church in Flushing, a noted stop on the Underground Railroad. This lithograph is believed to be a memorial print made available to his parish shortly after his untimely death. (Weeksville Heritage Center.)

17

Berean Baptist Church, a racially mixed congregation in the once-neighboring black community of Carsville, was founded in 1850 and was a stop on the Underground Railroad. The church is still a viable presence at 1635 Bergen Street and is acknowledged as the first African American church in New York City to construct its own building from the ground up. This building was annexed in 1915 and 1961. (Berean Baptist Church.)

Rev. Simon Bundick, a former minister of Concord Baptist Church (1852–1856), also served as pastor of Berean Baptist Church in Weeksville. A victim of mental illness in his later years, he died in May 1879 in the Flatbush Asylum on the outskirts of Crown Heights. (Brooklyn Union Argus.)

Colored School No. 2, one of four in Brooklyn, was once located at the corner of Buffalo Avenue and Pacific Street. Junius C. Morel, the principal of Colored School No. 2 and head of the African Civilization Society, served both the school and local school system from 1847 until his death in 1874. (Weeksville Heritage Center.)

This holds up Segregated Schools in Brooklyn

PS 83 is historically recognized as the first integrated school in Brooklyn. In 1894, under a statute banning school segregation, the students at Colored School No. 2 were combined with their white student body thereby ending school segregation in the state. (Weeksville Heritage Center.)

A lone figure attempts to cross a near-deserted street as a trolley heads downhill toward the intersection of Nostrand Avenue and Malbone Street (now Empire Boulevard). The Kings County Penitentiary once stood at the left bend of this sparsely populated location. (Brian Merlis.)

The wooden planks and Belgian blocks that once paved the streets are gone, and this 1940s photograph of the same intersection captures a much busier and more urban setting. The intersection of Nostrand Avenue and Empire Boulevard is today one of the busiest and most congested corners in Crown Heights. (Brian Merlis.)

In this 1930s snapshot, two quaint frame structures with front porch and picket fence stand along the last remaining fragment of the old Clove Road, a pre-Revolutionary thoroughfare that once connected the old town of Bedford to the township of Flatbush. The houses are shadowed by a six-story brick apartment building, and PS 161 can also be seen in the distance. (New York City Municipal Archives.)

Trolley tracks defy the challenges of uphill construction at this intersection of Kingston Avenue at Empire Boulevard in 1923. Trolley tracks remain embedded in the ground in today's Brooklyn and were simply covered with asphalt when electric-run buses were replaced first by diesel and then gasoline-driven energy. (Brian Merlis.)

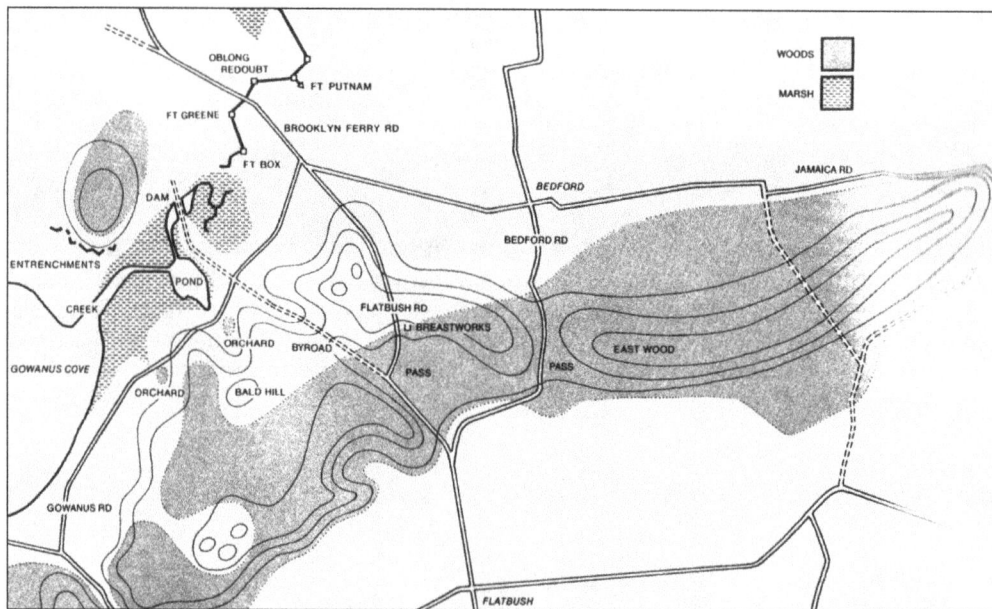

The closely placed rings and deep shading indicate the high altitudes and dense woods that flank the cleft labeled here as the Bedford Road, also known as the Clove Road. The woods and marsh delineated on this map documents the physical challenges of living and farming in early Crown Heights. (The David Library of the American Revolution.)

This 1930s shot captures a small frame home with flagpole and resident goat (left of picket fence) next to the compelling poster message to purchase Edelbrau beer. Once part of a row of similarly constructed homes that sat on Bergen Street near today's Eastern Parkway extension, the unit was removed in 2006. (New York City Municipal Archives.)

A row of prefabricated homes have replaced the old frame home, with the only surviving house from that era still standing on the far right (white top). A multifamily building in the rear was erected more than 30 years ago.

The 23th Regiment Armory at Pacific Street and Bedford Avenue defines the location of this well-developed block where a freestanding mansion is set back from its wrought-iron gate. The landmarked St. Bartholomew's Anglican Church (not visible) is found at the end of this block, just a few yards from the armory. (Brian Merlis.)

No trace of the mansion is in evidence in this 2009 image. The apartment building (with fire escapes) now occupies the space next to the once-peaked structure next door. That architectural feature was removed, and an additional fourth story was added to the formerly three-story building.

Two

INSTITUTIONS
AND SERVICES

The raw, undeveloped land of early and underpopulated Crown Heights made it a perfect place for 19th-century institutions looking to establish new or replacement facilities. Remote and affordable, it attracted a plethora of orphanages, hospitals, homes for the aged and infirmed, an armory, truant home, almshouse, monastery, and even a penitentiary during a remarkable era of social awareness.

Some of these included the St. John's Home for Boys at St. Mark's Place and Albany Avenue (1868); the Orphan Asylum of the City of Brooklyn, Kingston and Atlantic Avenues (1872); the Hebrew Orphanage, Ralph Avenue and Pacific Street (1879); Howard Colored Orphanage, Dean Street and Troy Avenue (1866); St. Joseph's Home for the Deaf, Buffalo Avenue and Bergen Street (1850); Monastery of Carmelite Nuns, Bedford Avenue and Lincoln Place (1907); Truant Home on Clove Road, now Empire Boulevard and Nostrand Avenue (1857); Brooklyn Penitentiary, Nostrand Avenue and Crown Street (1848); and the Zion Home for Colored Aged, St. John's Place and Kingston Avenue (1869).

A multitude of hospitals once served the public at a time when money was scarce, but treatment was available to almost all who required it. These included St. Mary's Hospital, Buffalo Avenue and Bergen Street (1882); Brooklyn Jewish Hospital, Classon Avenue and Prospect Place (1902); Home for Nervous Invalids, 883 St. Mark's Avenue; Kings County Asylum for Chronic Insane and Alms House; Home for Habitues, Brooklyn Avenue near Park Place (1902) for the opium, chloral, and cocaine addicted; House of St. Giles the Cripple, President Street and Brooklyn Avenue (1891); Brooklyn's Women's Hospital, Eastern Parkway and St. John's Place; Lefferts General Hospital, Brooklyn Avenue and East New York Avenue (1906); Carson Peck Memorial, Crown and Albany Avenues (1919); Swedish Hospital, 1350 Bedford Avenue (1906); Unity Hospital, 1545 St. John's Place; Thoracic Hospital, St. John's Place and Kingston Avenue; and House of the Good Shepherd (1868), on the extreme outskirts of the neighborhood.

A last remaining example of these once grand facilities can be found at St. Mark's Place between Brooklyn and New York Avenues. Formerly a Methodist Episcopal home for men and founded in 1890, a Seventh-Day Adventist school now inhabits the space.

Penitentiary convicts dressed in traditional penal garb—stripped suit, vest, and cap—assemble for a day of labor. Many Brooklyn roads and foundations for public buildings were dug using 19th-century prison manpower during the active expansion and settlement of the borough's rural areas. By the 1930s, every state had abolished the practice of leasing convict labor. (Brooklyn Public Library Brooklyn Collection.)

This 24th ward map shows the penitentiary's footprint before it closed in 1907. Encompassing two full city blocks and flanked by Nostrand and Rogers Avenues, while bounded on the north by President Street, the prison's entrance faced Crown Street. Few buildings surrounded the institution at that time, and only a proposed grid for future homes existed. The diagonal pathway of the ancient Clove Road (above the penitentiary) is still delineated. (New York City Municipal Archives.)

Founded in nearby Flatbush in the 1830s as an extension of the Brooklyn Hospital and Almshouse, the Kings County Penitentiary moved to this Crown Heights structure in 1846. It once held from 600 to 1,000 prisoners in its 11-acre facility.

In 1848, it is estimated that 10,000 children never attended school but instead lived on the street. To survive, many gathered rags and refuse papers, sold toothpicks and matches, were newsboys or organ grinders, and slept in boxes, old wagons, or on the pavement over printing vaults. (Public domain.)

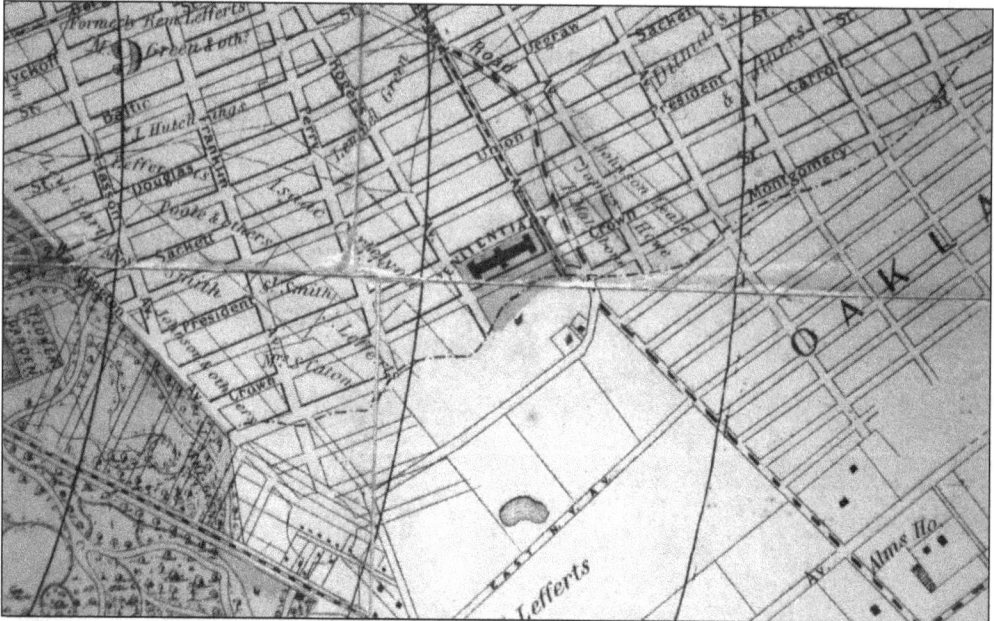

To meet the needs of vagrant, neglected, and homeless children in New York, a Truant Home was opened in December 1857 to insure their care and instruction. The original truant buildings are shown on the above map, directly south of the penitentiary. It was originally a tavern, as well as an even-earlier home of the prison. Built of wood and standing two stories high, it was surrounded by a high board fence and held about 120 children, until moving to new facilities in East New York in 1869. (Brooklyn Public Library Brooklyn Collection.)

Brooklyn to Have Jesuit College and Church

Following the prison's closing and transfer of inmates to Blackwell's Island in February 1907, the Society of Jesus purchased the former prison grounds for construction of this proposed structure to house a Catholic College and Preparation School. Although only a small part of the much simpler college building had been completed, the school formally opened in September 1908 with 200 students enrolled. During its 64-year history, over 8,500 men were graduated from the institution. (Brooklyn Archdiocese.)

Acquired by the City of New York in 1970, today this site is home to Medgar Evers College, an accredited four-year institution and a part of the City University of New York (CUNY). Named in honor of the slain civil rights leader Medgar Wiley Evers, the school offers a variety of outstanding degree programs.

The steeple of the Roman Catholic church of St. Gregory the Great (established in 1905) is shown under construction on the corner of Brooklyn Avenue and St. John's Place. Located only a few blocks from St. Matthew's Roman Catholic Church (established in 1886), at Utica Avenue and Eastern Parkway, and near St. Ignatius Roman Catholic Church (established in 1908), the churches met the spiritual needs of the large Irish, German, and Italian population living in the neighborhood. (Brian Merlis.)

Bishop McDonnell Memorial High School for Girls, which opened in 1926, was located on Eastern Parkway and Classon Avenue in the western boundaries of Crown Heights. Named in memory of Brooklyn's first Bishop, the Right Reverend Charles E. McDonnell (1892–1921), the Right Reverend Thomas E. Molloy (1922–1956) succeeded Bishop McDonnell. The high school closed in 1974 and is today St. Francis de Sales School for the Deaf, serving children ages 5–15. (Brooklyn Archdiocese.)

St. Gregory the Great Roman Catholic Church in 2009 (shown above), still strikingly beautiful and well maintained, serves parishioners of predominant Caribbean and African descent. This view was taken looking north on Brooklyn Avenue facing St. John's Place. (Brooklyn Archdiocese.)

31

St. Matthew's Roman Catholic Church, founded in 1886, was originally opened as a mission chapel located on Schenectady Avenue between Montgomery and Crown Streets. Under the leadership of the church's first pastor, Fr. James P. O'Boyle, and then Fr. Patrick J. McGlinchey, a more spacious church and rectory were established in 1893 on Lincoln Place (formerly Degraw Street) and Utica Avenue. (Brooklyn Archdiocese.)

The old rectory (left) became St. Matthew's School when a new parcel of land, which conveniently extended through to Lincoln Place, was acquired in 1912. The parishioners themselves leveled the hill on the raw property, and it is in this location that the present structure stands today. The new St. Matthew's edifice was dedicated on a Sunday in May 1914. (Brooklyn Archdiocese.)

The first graduate of St. Matthew's School, Anne McCabe, received this certificate in June 1893 for her, "Diligent and earnest study, punctual attendance, and correct deportment." Its elegant graphics are a bow to the fastidious formality observed during that era. (Brooklyn Archdiocese.)

One year later, in June 1894, the first group of St. Matthew's graduates poses for its commencement picture. After 80 years, the parish school closed in 1973 under a consolidation effort of the Brooklyn Archdiocese. (Brooklyn Archdiocese.)

The Monastery of Our Lady of Mount Carmel was at the corner of Bedford Avenue and Lincoln Place in Crown Heights for more than 90 years (1907–1997). The Carmelite nuns once lived in this cloister in a routine of prayer and contemplation until maintenance costs and increasing urbanization forced them to move. (New York City Municipal Archives.)

The thick walls of the former monastery have been removed, and the space is today a complex of newly renovated cooperative apartments. The beautiful lines of the monastery's architecture can now be appreciated by all passersby.

This view of the Gen. Henry W. Slocum memorial statue, installed in 1905 on Eastern Parkway and Bedford Avenue, depicts the stark, undeveloped environment of the young thoroughfare. Only saplings grace the avenue, and open fields still define the now highly urbanized location. (Brooklyn Public Library Brooklyn Collection.)

This Brooklyn Home for the Aged, shown today on the corner of St. John's Place and Kingston Avenue, was founded in Weeksville in 1869 by the Zion AME Church in Manhattan under the name Zion Home for Colored Aged. Once the next-door neighbor of the Howard Colored Orphanage on Dean Street between Albany and Troy Avenues (once located on Ralph Avenue and Pacific Street), it has inhabited this site since 1900 when Booker T. Washington was the guest speaker at the building's opening ceremony.

Located on the northeastern corner of the same intersection as the Home for Colored Aged, the Thoracic Hospital for Consumptives on Kingston Avenue and St. John's Place specialized in the treatment of tuberculosis. The huge facility occupied a full half block in an area once considered an ideal rural retreat for patients with lung disease. (Brian Merlis.)

The Thoracic Hospital's fronting on St. John's Place, shown here, was torn down years ago, but only recently built upon. Multifamily apartments, expected to be completed in 2009, will now occupy that space. (New York City Municipal Archives.)

The Brooklyn Swedish Hospital at Rogers Avenue and Sterling Place was founded in 1906 and served the local population from a complex of three adjoining buildings including the Victorian structure with mansard roof shown here. Odessa Home for the Aged moved into the building after the hospital built new facilities at Bedford Avenue and Dean Street in 1939. This hospital closed its doors permanently in 1975. (New York City Municipal Archives.)

The Swedish Hospital was equipped with the latest mode of transporting patients in the 1930s. Here the ambulance driver and two hospital workers pose for a snapshot along Bedford Avenue and Eastern Parkway, just a short distance from the medical facility. The hospital's location is printed on the car door. (Brian Merlis.)

This nondescript, three-story structure on Rogers Avenue was a part of the three-building complex of the original Swedish Hospital. In 1939, the medical facility moved a few blocks north to a new and more modern building at Bedford Avenue and Pacific Street. Today this original structure houses a church school serving grades one to eight. (New York City Municipal Archives.)

Ongoing fund-raising efforts, headed by Rev. James H. Gordon, provided much-needed monies for the Howard Orphanage and Industrial School both in its Brooklyn location and later at its Kings Park, Long Island, home. All-girl quartets performed at teas, dinners, and bazaars at a variety of halls, churches, and Masonic temples in Brooklyn and Long Island and at ongoing dinners and luncheons, bringing critical funds to continue the institution. (Linda M. Jones.)

Rev. James H. Gordon, superintendant of the Howard Orphanage and Industrial School from May 1903 to March 1914, passed away while still holding office at the institute. A special memorial service was held for him at Bethany Baptist Church, then at Claremont and Atlantic Avenues, on April 21 of that year. The memorial program was adorned with the orphanage logo of two children in silhouette holding hands, subtitled, "To Give a Child a Chance." (Linda M. Jones.)

In the 1860s, when almost all aspects of Brooklyn life were segregated by race, ethnicity, and religion, the orphan homes were no exception. The Howard Colored Orphanage, originally founded in 1866 by Mrs. S. A. Tillman as the Home for Freed Children and Others, this three-story Coloburg brick building at Dean Street and Troy Avenue was constructed through the leadership and fund-raising efforts of its superintendant Rev. W. F. Johnson. First housed at Pacific Street and Ralph Avenue, they later attained the acreage and raised the funds to construct the new three-story home. The New York City Transit Division purchased the space when the orphanage moved to Kings Park, Suffolk County, Long Island, demolishing the structure and transforming it into a carbarn for trolleys. (Weeksville Heritage Center.)

The Brooklyn Orphan Asylum at Kingston and Atlantic Avenues was run by the Orphan Asylum Society of the City of Brooklyn. Founded in 1833 under the direction of Ann Sands and other prominent Brooklyn Heights residents, it was committed to orphans and children of destitute widows and prospered with the support of "kind persons . . . with liberal hand(s)." The asylum moved to the this building at Atlantic and Kingston Avenues in 1872. The opening ceremony was dedicated by the Revs. Henry Ward Beecher and N. H. Schenck, prominent ministers of their day. (New York City Municipal Archives.)

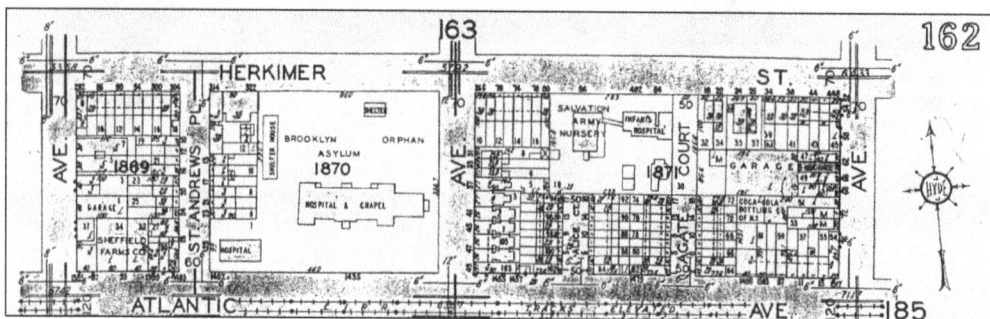

The Brooklyn Orphan Asylum at 1435 Atlantic Avenue was located one block from the Salvation Army Nursery off Agate Court and across Atlantic Avenue from the Brooklyn Training School and Home for Young Girls. The orphanage's 3.38-acre space was bought by New York City in 1945 and is today the St. Andrew's Playground. (New York City Municipal Archives.)

The House of St. Giles the Cripple, an orthopedic hospital located on the corner of President Street and Brooklyn Avenue, was founded in 1891 by Sister Sarah, an Episcopalian nun. It moved to this location in 1916, which coincided with the year of the great polio epidemic. The 1954 discovery of the Salk vaccine diminished the need for this convalescent home. It was sold in 1973 to the St. Mark Episcopal Church to house its elementary school. (New York City Municipal Archives.)

The St. Mark's Day School is the educational arm of the St. Mark Episcopal Church located one block away on the corner of Brooklyn Avenue and Union Street. The parochial school is now entering its 26th year at this location.

The Squadron C Armory, at Bedford Avenue between Union and President Streets, is a short distance from a second structure—the 23rd Regiment Armory—located only a few blocks north, also located in Crown Heights. It was created to house the National Guard and Civilian Infantry and is led by the New York State governor. (Brian Merlis.)

A statue of Gen. Henry W. Slocum was positioned at Eastern Parkway and Bedford Avenue, facing west toward Franklin Avenue and located within the shadow of the Squadron C (formerly known as Troop C) Armory. Today the statue is stationed within shrubbery adjacent to the Grand Army Plaza Arch of Triumph and facing the Brooklyn Public Library's main branch. (Brian Merlis.)

44

Development continues in 1923 at the corner of Troy and Crown Streets as new multifamily apartment buildings rise across the street from the new Carson C. Peck Memorial Hospital. Set on "high ground, [and] overlooking the city with a glimpse of distant water," the January 13, 1919, hospital opening was reviewed by the *New York Times* as "a fine product of intelligence and skill." This image of Carson C. Peck Memorial captures its grandeur. (Brian Merlis.)

Upon entering the portals of Carson C. Peck Memorial Hospital, one ascended to the grandeur of the then technologically advanced institution lavishly constructed of stained glass, marble, and brick. Named in remembrance of Carson C. Peck, a vice president and treasurer of the F. W. Woolworth Company and owner of the *Brooklyn Daily Times* who died at age 57 in Brooklyn, the hospital's construction was financed by Peck's widow, Clara Sargent Peck, who died in 1928. (Public domain.)

The Hebrew orphan home at Ralph Avenue and Pacific Street housed Jewish orphans and half orphans but did not always have a parochial school attached to it. As late as the 1930s, "inmates" (as they were called) dressed in their starched and pressed orphanage uniforms would attend nearby St. Claire McKelway Junior High School 178.

Neighboring Flatbush shares history, heritage, culture, and real estate ownership with the northern communities of Crown Heights and Bedford-Stuyvesant. Here at Bedford and Church Avenues, and next to historic Erasmus Hall High School, the Flatbush School No. 1, built 1878–1894, became the Brooklyn Yeshiva University Boy's High School from 1954 to 1967 and Beth Rivka Institute for girls from 1968 to 1990. Many who attended lived in Crown Heights. Since its closure in the 1990s, the landmarked building has been allowed to deteriorate. (Public domain.)

46

Formerly a synagogue, the Universal Temple Church of God, located at Eastern Parkway (left) and Lincoln Place, reflects the changes in demographics during the 1960 and 1970s. The Star of David can still be seen at the top of the wedge-shaped building.

The former home of a local Jewish Reformed congregation, the magnificent domed Schaare Zedek Synagogue bears the words "Gates of Righteousness" in both English and Hebrew on its parapet. Today the First Church of God in Christ resides here at 221 Kingston Avenue and Park Place.

Beautifully renovated as a triplex dwelling in 2006, this three-story freestanding building at Park Place and New York Avenue was purchased in 1941 to house a private institution, the Brooklyn Community School. Originally a one-family dwelling owned by Mrs. B. Gillis, a building medallion now bears the descriptive wording, "The Mansion."

LEFFERTS J. H. S. 61, B'KLYN

The rectangular, glass-and-steel Lefferts Junior High School No. 61 on Empire Boulevard and New York Avenue is in stark contrast with the elegant lines of the private Brooklyn Community School. Constructed in the late 1950s, it once bore the name of one of the largest landholding families in Bedford, Crown Heights, and Flatbush. It is now the Gladstone H. Atwell Intermediate School.

The George W. Wingate secondary school, although just beyond the neighborhood borders in what some refer to as East Flatbush, was nonetheless the assigned high school of Crown Heights 9th through 12th graders. Shaped like a banjo and installed at 600 Kingston Avenue in the 1950s, its stark lines are similar to the Lefferts Junior High School building nearby.

This rare 1944 graduation program of PS 161, built in 1924 on Crown Street just east of Clove Road, depicts the local school, then headed by principal Arthur J. Stang. The program front includes the statement, "America Is a Nation, One Flag – One Language – One Loyalty," a quote credited to Theodore Roosevelt. (Brian Merlis.)

Viewed through the chain-link fence that now surrounds the landmarked Weeksville Houses (not shown), the refurbished church structure and remnant stone wall (left) are modern reminders of the 1930s Weeksville at the Buffalo Avenue and Bergen Street intersection, shown below and on page 51.

Surrounded by a brick wall, at this Bergen Street and Buffalo Avenue intersection, was the St. Joseph's School for the Deaf at 113 Buffalo Avenue, which was administered by the Brooklyn Roman Catholic Archdiocese. (New York Public Library.)

Only the retaining rubble wall remains of the St. Joseph's School for the Deaf that once resided in Weeksville. The street has been reconfigured with traffic now redirected around the massive Kingborough housing complex constructed by New York City in 1941 and housing more than 2,300 people.

This African American church at Bergen Street and Buffalo Avenue was once known as the Buffalo Methodist Episcopal Church and noted as a recognized landmark of the original Weeksville community. The Church of God in Christ on the Hill is now housed at this location and today faces the renovated Weeksville houses (not shown) dating back to the 19th century. Trolley tracks and aerial copper coated electric power lines date this picture to the 1920s. (New York Public Library.)

This Carnegie library sits at the juncture of Eastern Parkway and Schenectady Avenue, across the street from PS 167. The home-away-from-home for many local students over the years, this two-story, five-bay edifice is one of 21 individual branches constructed through an 1892 endowment from Andrew Carnegie, of which 18 Brooklyn Carnegies still operate as libraries today.

In 2009, after a recent steam cleaning, PS 167, also known as the Parkway School, appears to be almost new. It instructs prekindergarten to grade five students from this location at 1025 Eastern Parkway and is the source of many fond memories, as evidenced by the warm and lively remembrances of "167 bloggers."

The intersection of Eastern Parkway and Schenectady Avenue has seen many changes over the years. Surrounded by rough dirt roads, horse-drawn wagons, and the rare jalopy, PS 167 (right), towers above the small frame houses and low-rise brick buildings that surround it. (New York Public Library.)

Here in a more urban 1930s image, the Eastern Parkway in the foreground has been beautifully paved, and an underground train system has been installed, evidenced by a convenient subway entrance in front of the school. A newspaper vendor is also stationed outside the school. (Brooklyn Public Library Brooklyn Collection.)

The Methodist Episcopal Home for the Aged at Park Place and New York Avenue was incorporated in 1883, dedicated in 1889, and housed 60 inmates. It once cared for men over the age of 65 years and who were members of the Methodist church for 10 years. The admission fee was $100, and any property was secured by the home before admittance. Covered in ivy, the original building is shown here. (Brian Merlis.)

Annexed over the years, the original building spire is now located in the center of the structure. It is located on Park Place between New York and Brooklyn Avenues and represents the only neighborhood building still standing today that once housed one of an extraordinary number of benevolent institutions. Today it is the Hebron School run by the Seventh-Day Adventist Church.

Three

PEOPLE AND PLACES

Today's Crown Heights was once a collection of smaller townships, each functioning as separate and independent entities. Although recognized as part of the larger Brooklyn community, each was an identifiable hamlet in its own right. These included not only the African American township of Weeksville but also the now-forgotten locations of Malboneville; the Crow Hill community between Albany and Schenectady Avenues in the Green Mountains of central Brooklyn, home to an entrenched population of squatters; Carsville northeast of Weeksville; and Pigtown, south of Montgomery Street and New York Avenue, and later designated as Oakland. Noted as a strongly united Italian community, its unofficial mayor, Tom Colandirello, successfully orchestrated Pigtown's local voting block.

Over the years, many brilliant, talented, and ultimately famous people emerged from these streets, including the celebrated record producer and multiple Grammy Award winner Clive Davis; entertainer Stephanie Mills; jazz violinist Noel Pointer; his mother, Broadway star and educator Louvinia G. Pointer; singer/actor Ronnie Dyson; the pop group Crown Heights Affair; and Grammy winner Corey Glover.

This remarkable urban epicenter is also home to Abraham Beame, who later became mayor of New York City; New York State Assembly Speaker Stanley Steingut; first black congress woman and presidential candidate Shirley Chisolm; and slain New York City councilman James Davis, to name just a few.

Literary talent John Killens nurtured the artistic gift of Maya Angelou from his home on Union Street; and his neighbor humorist Sam Levenson, lived just doors away. Erich Segal, author of the book and cinema hit *Love Story* grew up at 800 St. Mark's Avenue within a short walk of Killens.

The people and places in Crown Heights represent the remarkable and vibrant nature of a dynamic, multicultural neighborhood. It defies the labeling by the media and politicians who identify its homes and people as residents of the inner city. Its deep history is not an afterthought or an insignificant cog that helps make Manhattan run.

Crown Heights is, and remains, an American location of beauty and promise, with a dynamic history that is, and hopefully continues to be, a glowing example of multicultural successes and unlimited accomplishment.

Arguably the most famous of Brooklyn landmarks, the old Ebbets Field stadium was home to remarkable players like Jackie Robinson, Phil Rizzutto, Roger Maris, and Yogi Berra to name only a few. Demolished in 1972, to make way for an apartment complex, the delicate tracery of artist Christopher Nesbit marks the exact location of the old home of the long-missed and never forgotten Brooklyn Dodgers. (Christopher Nesbit.)

Facing north on Franklin Avenue toward the Fulton Street elevated line, this 1921 image is just outside the Crown Heights border at Atlantic and Franklin Avenues. This maze of elevated steel and overhead bridge ways was an important transfer point for riders heading south toward Brooklyn's shores. (Brian Merlis.)

Viewed from inside the train terminal, this Brooklyn line commencing at the Franklin Avenue and Fulton Street junction took riders to nearby Ebbets Field and Prospect Park or more distantly to the Brighton Beach and Coney Island shores. Now diminished to a two-car, five-stop shuttle service, it provides essential convenience for the neighborhoods of Bedford-Stuyvesant, Crown Heights, and Flatbush, all within its short 15-minute run. (Brian Merlis.)

The Carmelite nuns, who took vows of silence and lived devout lives of prayer and meditation, moved to this monastery in 1907, when Crown Heights was a sparsely populated, almost rural location. The Sisters of Carmel moved in 1983. Here in a 2009 image, the walls have been removed, and the space is now a condominium.

In the 1870s, following the conclusion of the Civil War, construction was completed on a magnificent plaza on the outskirts of Crown Heights, with an arch (left) dedicated to the victorious triumph of the Union's Grand Army of the Republic. The Brooklyn Museum (far right), newly completed in 1897, sits on the elevation of Prospect Hill, and the Reservoir Tower marks the location of the public water system. (Public domain.)

Nine Civil War veteran soldiers, accompanied by a marching band, lead the procession down Eastern Parkway, followed by companies of the 106th, 107th, and 108th Infantry in 1925. Photographed at the corner of Brooklyn Avenue, the old reservoir water tower (right) can be seen in the distance, with the Brooklyn Museum building to its left. Half the Eastern Parkway was evidently left available for automobile traffic heading west for the convenience of the drivers. In

the distance, one of the many formidable hills that are common to the once even hillier Crown Heights neighborhood can be seen. A parade on Decoration Day (later renamed Memorial Day) along Eastern Parkway was an annual activity from the 1920s through the 1960s. Many members of the "Greatest Generation" recall the last Civil War soldiers being driven along the parade route in limousines once they were too elderly to march. (New York Public Library.)

Crown Heights resident and religious leader, the late rabbi Menachem Mendel Schneerson (1902–1994) headed the Chabad-Lubavitch movement of Chasidic Judaism for 44 years. Migrating from Europe to New York in 1941 to escape religious persecution, Rabbi Schneerson came to lead the growth of the Lubavitch community from a small movement, to a worldwide community of 200,000 members. (Public domain.)

Folksinger and songwriter Bob Dylan, born Robert Zimmerman, reportedly worshipped with the Crown Heights Lubavitch community and was, per the New York Daily News, taking instruction from Talmudic scholars during the 1980s. The Chasidic community is the fastest growing demographic in the Crown Heights community and has spread from its Brooklyn roots to more than 110 countries worldwide. (Public domain.)

The headquarters of the Lubavitch movement is located at 770 Eastern Parkway and serves as a place of daily prayer services, a study hall for students, and assembly hall for Chabad gatherings. The structure has been replicated in Jerusalem, Israel, and Australia, and near-replicas have been built in New Jersey, Los Angeles, Cleveland, Milan, Rio de Janeiro, and Buenos Aires.

As much a fixture in the old Brooklyn neighborhoods as Dubrow's Cafeteria or the bakery chain Ebingers, Lofts candy outlets and Cushman's bake goods were frequented by a community that enjoyed their produce and still waxes nostalgic at the mention of the old Brooklyn food outlets. (New York City Municipal Archives.)

The first Dubrow's Cafeteria was established at this Crown Heights location at Eastern Parkway and Utica Avenue in 1929. Founded by Benjamin Dubrow, who was a native of Belarus, he added an additional restaurant on Kings Highway and East Sixteenth Street in Brooklyn and expanded his chain to include locations in Manhattan and Miami Beach. (Brian Merlis.)

A popular meeting place for locals and businessmen, presidents John F. Kennedy and Jimmy Carter, Sen. Robert Kennedy, and New York governor Hugh Corey chose both the Brooklyn and Manhattan locations as stumping grounds for their political campaigns. Dubrow's closed its last restaurant in Manhattan's Garment District in 1985. (Brian Merlis.)

The Church of St. Mark Episcopal on the corner of Brooklyn Avenue and Union Street abuts the newly constructed homes of "Spotless Town," a forerunner of today's gated communities. The spacious three-story buildings at one time shared a single, emissions-controlled generator, which limited ash and soot from fouling the air; a remarkable innovation at that time. (Brian Merlis.)

Humorist and Brooklyn-native Sam Levenson (left, with his daughter) lived on that block until the 1970s. A teacher, author, and early television personality, Levenson was a 1950s panelist on *What's My Line*, with (from left to right) Jane Meadows, Lee Bowman, and Faye Emerson. The advertisers Green Mint and Py-co-pay were truly ever-present sponsors. (Brooklyn College Special Collections.)

In 2009, the sycamores now tower over the "Spotless Town" block on Union Street, home to Sam Levenson, as well as the noted writer, educator, and activist John Oliver Killens. A champion of civil rights, Killens participated in the historic march on Washington on August 28, 1963. Grace Killens, his widow, and family still live in the family home.

John O. Killens (1900–1987) was a gifted writer whose talent showed itself in his early childhood. This remarkable gift was in fact mistaken for plagiarism by his fifth-grade teacher when Killens was growing up in Georgia. After serving in World War II, he went on to write the award winning *Youngblood*, as well as Pulitzer Prize nominated *And Then We Heard the Thunder* (1963) and *The Cotillion* (1971). He is shown here at a 1974 Howard University writer's conference with actor, singer, and activist Harry Belafonte (left). (Barbara Killens-Rivera.)

A nurturer of talent, John O. Killens helped found and chaired the Harlem Writers Guild and gave direction to students seeking to hone their skills. Here he is with Neari Evans (right, in cap) and Maya Angelou (far right), also a resident of Crown Heights, and five students of Medgar Evers College, part of the State University of New York (SUNY) located in the neighborhood. (Barbara Killens-Rivera.)

The Civil War service of Union general Henry Warner Slocum (1827–1894) was honored by Brooklyn residents with the commission of a statue designed by sculptor Frederick MacMonnies. A veteran of many battles including Bull Run, Antietam, and Gettysburg, Slocum was a native New Yorker from Onondaga County but chose Brooklyn as his adoptive home in his final years. (New York Public Library.)

The 1902 unveiling of the General Slocum statue, installed at Eastern Parkway and Bedford Avenue, was presided over by Pres. Theodore Roosevelt and celebrated with a parade of schoolgirls carrying flags, marching bands, and celebratory bunting. Visible is the Troop C Armory, still standing today at Union Street and Bedford Avenue, although now partially hidden by nearby buildings. The statue is installed in the Grand Army Plaza circle.

Located at the corner of Empire Boulevard and New York Avenue, this old-fashioned Esso gas station from the 1920s sits just yards from the old Clove Road (not seen), which was once the primary thoroughfare for travel from Bedford township to the Flatbush community. (New York City Municipal Archives.)

More than 70 years later in 2009, gasoline is still dispensed on the same corner, and the low one-story Beth and David Gershon Synagogue of Crown Heights also remains next to the station. The 71st police precinct is also still located across the street.

Joan Maynard (left), Weeksville Society executive director, led a group committed to preserving African American history and heritage in that township. Here she talks with Alex Haley (light suit), neighborhood resident Dr. Vernal Cave, and Audrey Phillips, president of the Weeksville Society. The successful work of saving the four remaining Weeksvile homes as landmarks continues to attract the attention of the city, state, and nation from its early efforts of the 1970s. (Weeksville Heritage Center.)

One of the many ongoing fund-raisers conducted for the Howard Colored Orphanage is announced by this 1914 flyer. Even with the move to Kings Park, Long Island, the orphanage was still very much rooted in Brooklyn. This event was hosted by Bethany Baptist Church when it was located downtown on Atlantic and Clermont Avenues. (Linda M. Jones.)

A Lincoln Mass Meeting

WILL BE HELD BY THE

COLORED CITIZENS
OF GREATER NEW YORK, ON

Thursday, February 12, 1914
AT 8 P. M., AT THE

BETHANY BAPTIST CHURCH
Cor. of Atlantic and Clermont Ave's., Brooklyn, N.Y.

Rev. Holland Powell, D. D., Pastor

For the benefit of the Howard Orphanage and Industrial School, Located at Kings Park, L. I.

Rev. Jas. H. Gordon, Superintendent

Hon. GEORGE WIBBECAN
Will preside

The principal speaker of the evening will be
Coun. JAS. L. CURTIS, of N.Y.City

Dr. O. M. Waller, will represent the Medical Fraternity of Brooklyn and Dr. E. P. Roberts, the Medical Fraternity of New York City.
Counsellor Francis F.Giles will represent the Lawyers of Brooklyn
Mr. George Harris will represent the Press of Greater New York
Rev. C. P. Cole, D. D., will represent the Clergy.
Mr. W. Frederick Trotman, will represent The Business Men
Mr. L. Hollingsworth Wood, President of the Board of Managers, will introduce the Presiding Officer.

Music will be furnished by the best choirs and select voices of the city,
Rev. JAMES H. GORDON, Superintendent, will speak of the work.

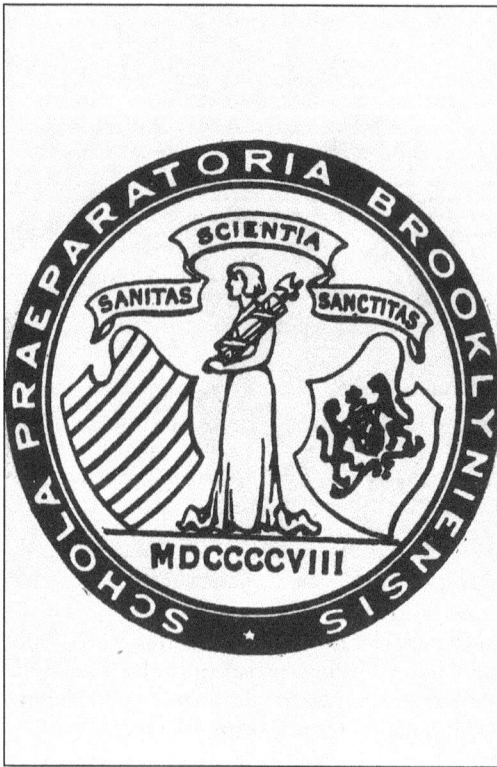

The Brooklyn Catholic Archdiocese played a large role in bringing architectural beauty and higher education to the Crown Heights community. Established in 1907, the Brooklyn Preparation School was first a college and then a preparatory school that taught and molded over 9,300 young men during its 63-year existence. The Brooklyn Prep School seal (left) stresses the values of religion, health, character, and intellect with the Latin inscription, "Sanitas, scientia, sanctitas." (Brooklyn Archdiocese.)

Joseph Paterno (class of 1945) attended Brooklyn Prep at Carroll Street and Nostrand Avenue, showing early promise in sports during his school years as team captain. He ultimately gained wide recognition as the head coach of the Pennsylvania State University's college football team, a position he has held since 1966, and was inducted in the College Football Hall of Fame in December 2007. (Brooklyn Archdiocese.)

JOSEPH PATERNO
Captain

Among the fine students who also graduated from this institution, William Blatty (class of 1945) became a world-renowned author with his release of the famous novel and cinema hit *The Exorcist*. (Brooklyn Archdiocese.)

WILLIAM J. BLATTY
Star of
Cyrano de Bergerac

Only two blocks west of the Brooklyn Preparation School, the Carroll Street footbridge (renovated in 1994) spans the Franklin Avenue shuttle tracks, while also providing a shortcut to the Brooklyn Botanic Gardens and the Brooklyn Museum at the westernmost boundary of the Crown Heights neighborhood.

A presence at 739 Eastern Parkway since 1972, the Vulcan Society, an organization for New York City African American firefighters, recognizes the valor, dedication, and bravery of its members. Following September 11, 2001, the Vulcan Society displayed the names and photographs of the 12 black firefighters who perished on that day. They were Andrew R. Fletcher, Keith Glascoe, Gerard L. Baptiste, Vernon Cherry, Karl Joseph, Leon Smith, Keithroy Maynard, Tarel Coleman, Vernon Richard, Ronnie Henderson, William L. Henry, and Shawn Powell. A total of 343 members of the New York City Fire Department were lost on 9/11, with a great many discovered long after the event.

Early Vulcan Society member fireman John W. Hamlin was recognized for his bravery in 1961 for saving the lives of two children. Hamlin received the Walter Scott Medal for his exceptional service and is being congratulated here by three-term (1954–1965) New York City mayor Robert F. Wagner Jr. (Dorothy Hamlin Rhodes.)

Celebration of Life and
Homegoing Service

Sunrise
August 29, 1928

Sunset
January 22, 2006

Joan Cooper Bacchus Maynard

Monday ~ January 30, 2006 ~ 6:30 P.M.

at

Frank R. Bell
Funeral Home, Inc.
536 Sterling Place
Brooklyn, New York 11238

OFFICIATING MINISTER:
The Reverend Dr. Johnny Ray Youngblood, Senior Pastor
Saint Paul Community Baptist Church
859 Hendrix Street
Brooklyn, New York 11207

"I am an empowering woman committed to the benefit of mankind." ~ Joan Maynard

Joan Cooper Bacchus Maynard (August 29, 1928–January 22, 2006) dedicated her talent, time, and energy to the preservation, historic designation, and operation of the resulting Society for the Preservation of Weeksville and Bedford-Stuyvesant History. A founding member in 1968, she was president from 1972 to 1974 and was the society's first executive director until her 1999 retirement. She remained executive director emeritus and ex officio trustee of the Weeksville board until her passing. A recipient of many awards, she received the Crowinshield Award in 1991, was a recipient of the Lucy G. Moses Preservation Award in 2004, and received the City of New York Mayor's Award for Art and Culture in the same year.

This is a late-winter 2009 photograph of the renovated Weeksville houses, 40 years after being saved from demolition.

Following the Great War, more than 2,000 memorial trees were dedicated to fallen soldiers along Eastern Parkway. At one time, each four-inch-by-nine-inch plaque honored individual dead. In spite of ongoing renovation, replantings, and even theft along the thoroughfare, many of these plaques can still be seen today. Here a memorial plaque with the green-patina of age states, "This tree is dedicated to the memory of Corp. Frank Bevers, Co. L. 308th Infantry, who died in the World War, 1914–1918."

The vernal qualities of the Eastern Parkway, constructed in the 1870s by Frederick Law Olmsted and Calvert Vaux, once provided light, shade, fresh air, and portable seating for locals seeking a period of leisure. Benches, now fastened to the Belgian walkways, were once untethered to allow patrons to adjust their view or exposure to the sun. Before heavy home and building construction, the Coney Island shore to the south provided delightful uphill ocean breezes that fanned the local residents during the heat of summer.

The first black policeman to work in the Weeksville 9th ward was Moses P. Cobb, a native of Kinston, North Carolina, and neighborhood homeowner. As did so many, Cobb came to New York for better educational and employment opportunities, and after working the waterfront, joined the force in 1892. He retired after 25 years of service in 1917. Here in 1983, Benjamin Ward (whose mother lived in Weeksville in the Howard Colored Orphanage) is named the first African American police commissioner by then mayor Edward I. Koch. (Public domain.)

Weeksville-native Dr. Susan Smith McKinney-Steward (1847–1918) was the first black woman physician in New York State and the third in the nation. She was a graduate of Manhattan's New York Medical College for Women (incorporated in 1863), the only place in New York City where women could study medicine. Dr. McKinney-Steward was the founder of the Womens Hospital and Dispensary, once located at 808 Prospect Place and Nostrand Avenue, and served as official physician for the Brooklyn Home for Aged Colored People on St. John's Place and Kingston Avenue. (Public domain.)

Local resident Shirley Chisholm (1924–2005) was the first black woman elected to Congress and in 1972 became the first major party black candidate for president of the United States on the Democratic ticket. Running successfully under the campaign slogan, "Un-bought and Un-bossed," Chisolm served the 12th congressional district for seven terms (1969–1983).

Brooklyn politicians of note who have represented Crown Heights over the years have included Charles Schumer, Al Vann, one-time neighborhood residents Stanley Steingut, and Abraham Beame (shown here). Once an active member of the Jewish Center on Eastern Parkway, Beame became New York City's first Jewish mayor and is noted for having overcome the $1.5 billion deficit in 1973 with a surplus of $200 million by the end of his term in 1977. He died at age 94 in 2001. (Public domain.)

December 30, 1916 - February 18, 2009

Louvinia G. Pointer (1917–2009), educator, Broadway star, and Crown Heights native, died at 92 and was widely mourned for her musical talent and related artistic accomplishments. Pointer worked with actor-playwrights Noel Coward and Ossie Davis, Alfred Lunt and Lynn Fontanne, and was praised by First Lady Eleanor Roosevelt for her work with the National Youth Administration Radio Workshop. Her son, Noel Pointer, a violin virtuoso and Grammy award nominee, predeceased her in 1994.

Record mogel, Grammy Award winner, and president of Arista Records, Clive Davis once lived one block from Shirley Chisholm on New York Avenue near President Street. A Brooklyn native, Harvard graduate, and member of the Rock and Roll Hall of Fame as a nonperformer, Davis has received renewed recognition with his recent appearances on the hit show *American Idol.* (New York Public Library.)

Four

REST AND RELAXATION

"All work and no play makes Jack a dull boy" is a familiar proverb of unknown source that dates back to 1659—a year that nearly coincides with the 1662 acquisition of Brooklyn acreage that eventually included today's Crown Heights and Weeksville neighborhoods.

From its earliest years, Colonial Brooklyn residents enjoyed seasonal Dutch celebrations such as *Pinkster* in the fall, and *Paasch* in the spring, followed in later years by follies, balls, sleigh rides, and ice-skating on nearby natural and manmade ponds. Horseback riding along the Clove Road was an enjoyable local pastime, with the 1870 development of Eastern Parkway providing its own unique avenue of entertainment and relaxation.

An extensive biking route, with connecting pathways from the Parkway in East New York to Coney Island, was created in the 1890s for the enjoyment of individual cyclists and avid cycling club enthusiasts.

In 1908, baseball club owner Charlie Ebbets began the consistent purchase of land parcels that, in five years, gained him ownership of an entire square block, later to become the famous Ebbets Field baseball stadium in 1913.

The Tammany Society funded picnics for the enjoyment of orphans, as well as beer and oyster galas for voters in the early 1900s. Boxing meets took place in Loyola Hall, a Brooklyn Prep building, now abutting Medgar Evers College. Local breweries abounded throughout Brooklyn at that time (producing more beer than Milwaukee), and beer gardens were popular places to relax.

Bedford Bowl later emerged as the sport hit its stride, and the popular Empire Rollerdrome served the roller-skating enthusiasts until its closure in 2007.

Local Yiddish live theater was replaced by movie houses like the Loew's Kameo and Carroll and Bedford theaters, which were followed by live entertainment and free concerts at Terrace Park and the Wingate Field.

Over the years, many neighborhood recreational sites have been lost to prefabricated housing and high-rise storage facilities, while population density has increased significantly. Nearby Manhattan recognized the importance of exercise and recreation in their August 1995 construction of Chelsea Piers 30-acre waterfront sports village, a space that offers bowling, skating, squash, golf, hockey, basketball, and roller-skating in one multistoried building. Crown Heights could use just such a space.

Brooklyn's Ebbets Field ballpark was known as a "hitter's paradise," a title evidently confirmed by this photograph of a third baseman heading toward home, as each man on the loaded bases advances. The stadium lighting and billboard advertisements for Schaefer beer and Lucky Strike cigarettes date this photograph back to the 1950s. (Brian Merlis.)

Ebbets Field opened on April 9, 1913, on a stretch of real estate once considered part of neighboring Flatbush but is today unquestionably part of Crown Heights. Bordered by Bedford Avenue, Sullivan Place, McKeever Place, and Montgomery Street, Charlie Ebbets acquired the one-block space as individual parcels came up for sale. Over the years, after suffering both prosperous and challenging times, player developer Branch Rickey signed Jackie Robinson in 1943, a move that broke the color line and brought the Brooklyn Dodgers a series of pennants and a World Series title in 1955. A dismounted policeman in front of the stadium tethers his horse, as a fellow officer watches the crowd file into the stadium in 1915. (Brian Merlis.)

Looking uphill on Brooklyn's Bedford Avenue, the crowded interior of Ebbets Field is clearly visible. Many who lived in apartment buildings overlooking the stadium enjoyed a great number of baseball games for free. Today the Ebbets Field apartments dominate the landscape. (Brian Merlis.)

The 1,500-seat Cameo Theater opened in 1924 and was renamed the Kameo when Loew's acquired it a year later. Located at Eastern Parkway and Nostrand Avenue, it once offered an open-air roof garden for the comfort of its patrons before the era of air conditioning. After its closure in 1973, it became the Philadelphian Sabbath Cathedral. A choice of other nearby theaters once included the Lincoln Place, Carroll on Utica Avenue, Empress on Empire Boulevard, as well as Werba's Riviera and Coronet both on St. John's Place, only a short walking distances for local residents. (New York City Municipal Archives.)

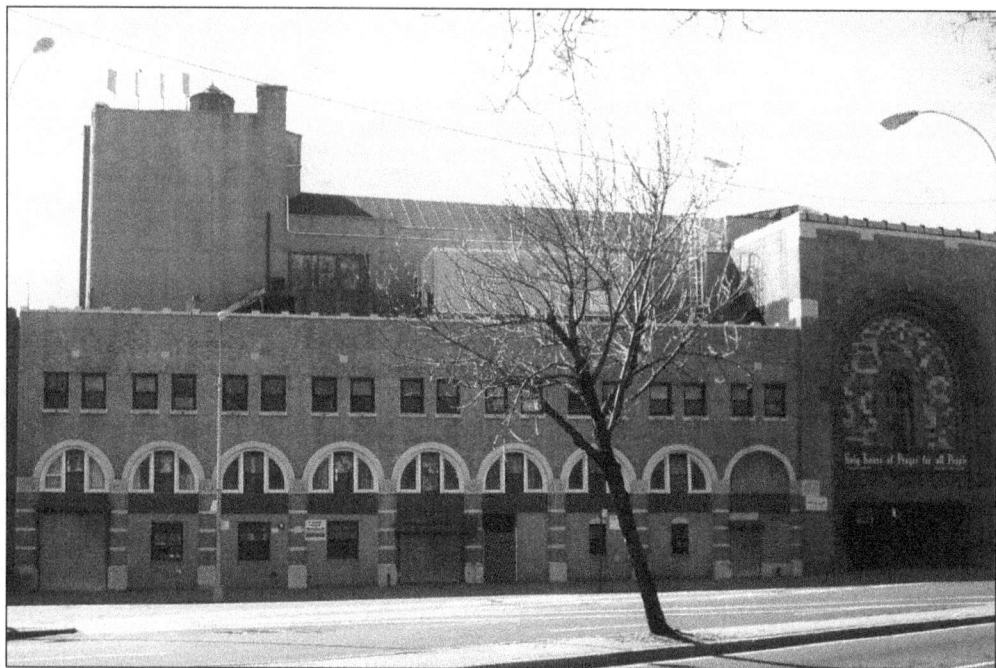

Live Yiddish theater was once performed here at this Eastern Parkway and Sterling Place location, including a reported appearance by the huge star Molly Picon. Situated on the eastern fringes of Weeksville and Crown Heights, it also borders on the once largely Jewish Brownsville and East New York neighborhoods of the 1930s, 1940s, and 1950s. The theater later replaced live entertainment with film. Today the church Holy House of Prayer for All People occupies the location.

The former theater on Bedford Avenue and Lincoln Place, off Eastern Parkway, is also now a church. The Charity Neighborhood Baptist Cathedral is located on an avenue that once housed the Carmelite Monastery, the old Swedish Hospital on Sterling Place, and the old Bedford Rest and subsequent Town Hill, all within a one-block proximity.

Loyola Hall (right), next to St. Ignatius Church (formerly St. Martin's Church) on Rogers Avenue and Crown Street, was a part of Brooklyn College (later the Brooklyn Preparatory School), administered by the Roman Catholic Jesuits from 1907 to 1970. The school's Brooklyn College Club participated in the amateur boxing tournaments held there during the 1920s. The hall is today part of the church and both are independent from Medgar Evers College, which bought the school buildings and grounds in 1970.

Over the years, a number of public halls in Crown Heights have transformed from popular pool halls to restaurant space for dining and dancing, to reception facilities for weddings and festive celebrations. This top floor space was once the Gayheart Ballroom at Eastern Parkway and Nostrand Avenue. Other local halls include the Franklin Manor Ballroom at Union Street and Franklin Avenue, with another located on Nostrand Avenue and Sterling Place.

Consumers Park Brewing Company produced this 1905 calendar depicting the actual structures that once stood at the Franklin Avenue and Montgomery Street addresses of the plant. A three-story building (right of the smoking stack structure), which still stands today, was once part of the brewing complex. Prohibition killed many of the more than 100 breweries that thrived in Brooklyn, once America's brewing capital, producing more beer than Milwaukee. (Brian Merlis.)

This remnant of Consumer Park Brewing is now covered in graffiti and visible above both the street fencing and from the Franklin Avenue shuttle train line that passes by the rear of the building many dozens of times each day. Consumer Park was also the name of a train station at Montgomery Street and the scene of a tragic train accident detailed in chapter 5 (page 108).

This photograph of the extant Consumer Park Brewing building, when viewed facing west, is dominated by the Ebbets Field Houses, former site of the Brooklyn Dodgers stadium. Plans are still unconfirmed regarding the future of this brewing structure, a last remnant of Brooklyn's once-glorious brewery history.

The Brooklyn Children's Museum, founded in 1899, was the first designed specifically for children. Located at Brooklyn and St. Mark's Avenues, the museum has resided in two different mansions within this vernal site (now known as Brower Park) and recently completed its most extensive renovation in September 2008, which doubled the institution's exhibit space to 102,000 square feet. (Brooklyn Public Library Brooklyn Collection.)

The Jewish Children's Museum at 332 Kingston Avenue and Eastern Parkway is a unique hands-on institution where children and their parents from all segments of the community can explore Jewish history and heritage. Founded in 1980 at the behest of Lubavitcher Rebbe and Rabbi Menachem M. Schnerson, and realized under the Tzivos Hashem International Children's organization's leadership, it opened in 2004.

A large, overscaled rendering of a child's dreidel adds a whimsical touch to the entrance of the Jewish Children's Museum, a 50,000-square-foot space dedicated to 16-year-old Ari Halberstam, who was killed in 1994 in a drive-by shooting on the entrance ramp to the Brooklyn Bridge by a terrorist.

91

The penny-farthing, or ordinary bicycle, was a French creation made of iron and wood with rubber tires and steel frame. It was difficult to ride due to its high seat and poor weight distribution. In 1885, the first recognizable modern bicycle was introduced, and by the 1890s, known as the golden age of bicycles, biking clubs for both men and women had become the rage.

A bicycle path along the Eastern Parkway was officially opened in 1893 for the many cycling enthusiasts that proliferated during that time. The pathway, a portion of which is shown here, swept along the Eastern Parkway, connected along the Ocean Parkway, and terminated at Coney Island. Here the 19th-century cyclists travel past the now-vanished reservoir and into the Grand Army Plaza.

The Green family is shown here in 1905 with their bicycles in front of their Weeksville home. Frank and Butsey are dressed for the sport with their trouser legs encased in their knee-high socks. (Weeksville Heritage Center.)

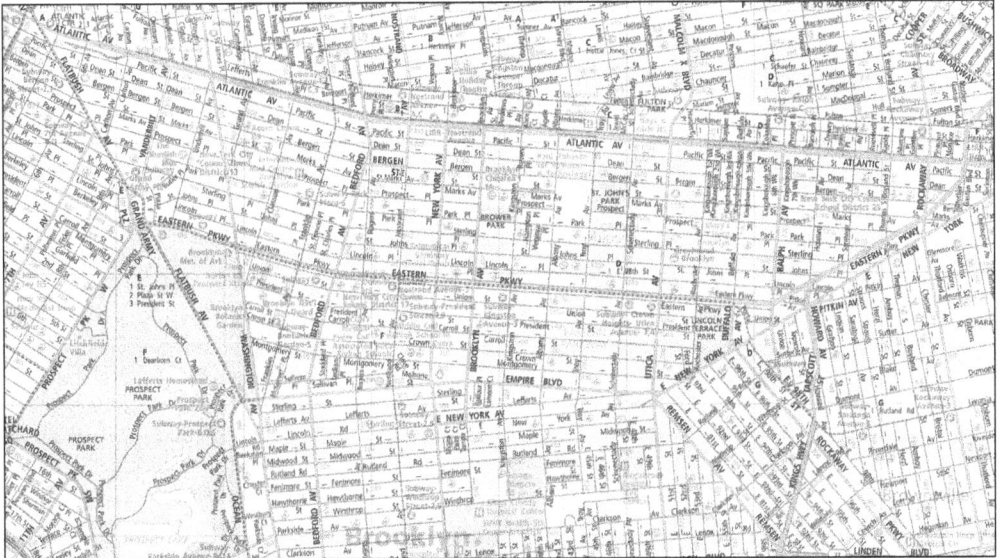

At the center of this map, running east to west, is the 2.2-mile Eastern Parkway thoroughfare. In fact, the entire Crown Heights area can be viewed, including the northern border of Atlantic Avenue and the prominent western boundary of Prospect Park.

The Bedford Hotel. Brooklyn, N. Y.

The Bedford Rest once stood at Eastern Parkway and Bedford Avenue, one of the highest elevations in Brooklyn in a neighborhood averaging 98 feet above sea level. Appropriately named, the restaurant (and here called a hotel) offered cyclists and locals food and refreshment before the Town Hill supper club was opened in its place by Morty Shnabel. (Brian Merlis.)

Sam Cooke (1931–1964), shown here in a recording session, was one of many singing stars to perform at the Town Hill Club in Crown Heights. It is reported that popular music producers Hugo Peretti and Luigi Creatore produced Cooke's hit "Chain Gang" after witnessing his magnetic after-hours performance at the club in 1960, which moved everyone, including the 3:00 a.m. closing-up waiters, to stop, sit, and listen. (Public domain.)

Town Hill

Supper Club

EXCELLENT CUISINE
DANCING
ENTERTAINMENT

·

3 SHOWS NIGHTLY, 10-12-2

Many of today's renowned performing artists, including Brook Benton, Della Reese, Sam Cooke, Jackie Wilson, and Ray Charles have appeared at the Town Hill sometime during their careers. It is said that Chubby Checker first performed "The Twist" at this venue, but the Peppermint Lounge got the credit. This souvenir photograph sleeve details the 10:00 p.m., 12:00 a.m., and 2:00 a.m. shows that were offered nightly. (Brian Merlis.)

Here Lloyd Price appears at Town Hill in the 1950s. Known for his hits, "Personality," "Lawdy Miss Clawdy," and "Stagger Lee," Price's long-lived career includes a recent tour with Jerry Butler, Gene Chandler, and Ben E. King for PBS television. (Brian Merlis.)

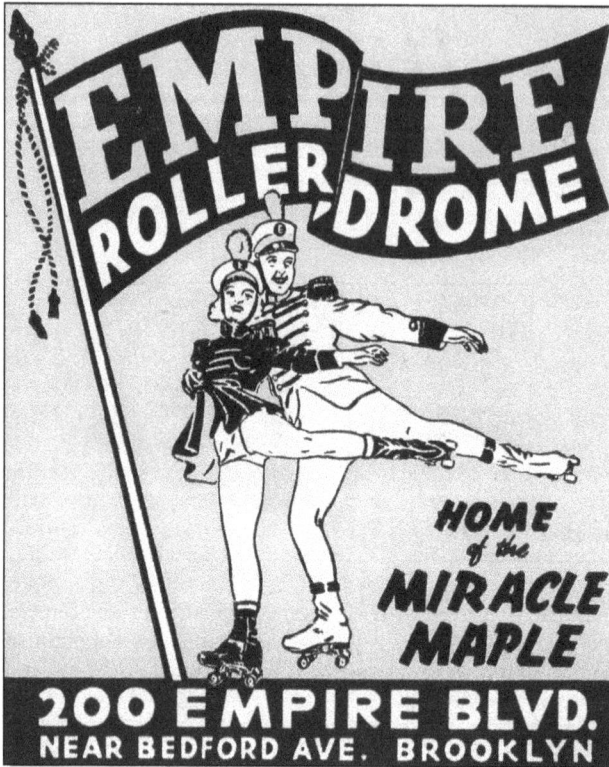

The Empire Rollerdrome rink, with its neon-lettered entryway, was the house of recreation for many generations of Brooklynites. Opened in the 1950s in what was formerly the parking garage of the Ebbets Field stadium, it provided a 50-year span of musical accompaniment, ranging from live organ music, then rock, and ultimately disco songs that drove the speed and dynamics of the skaters. (Brian Merlis.)

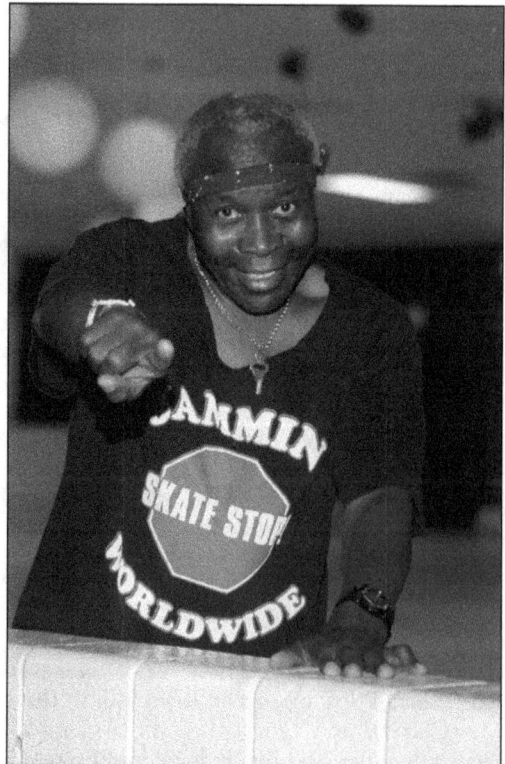

Professional skater Bill Butler, known widely as the "Godfather of Roller Disco," is credited with creating the Brooklyn Bounce at the Empire rink in the 1970s. This innovative skating style rooted in disco music made the Empire Rollerdrome known nationwide. At 75 years young, Butler still skates tournaments and exhibitions and now resides in Georgia. (Roller Skating Today.)

During his years as instructor, performer, and consultant at the Empire Rollerdrome, Bill Butler also escorted a number of celebrities who patronized the popular venue, including John F. Kennedy Jr., Paul Newman, and Ben Vereen. Here he guides superstar Cher around the rink during a Casablanca Records party in 1979. (Robin Platzer.)

EMPIRE ROLLERDROME
Home of the "Miracle Maple"

Special maple wood flooring made the surface of the Empire Rollerdrome especially conducive to smooth indoor roller-skating. A vintage postcard from the 1950s makes this point proclaiming the Empire Rollerdrome as the "Home of the 'Miracle Maple.'" (Brian Merlis.)

Rooted in 1920s Harlem, the annual West Indian Day parade has taken place along the Eastern Parkway thoroughfare from Utica Avenue to Grand Army Plaza in an annual celebration of Caribbean food, music, costumes, and culture every Labor Day Monday since 1967. Here the crowd surges past the Brooklyn Museum on Eastern Parkway. (Kenwin Lezama Jr.)

Founded by Carlos Lezama (1923–2007), who was born in South America and raised in Trinidad, the event has grown from a procession on Atlantic Avenue, to a parade along Bedford Avenue, and finally to an Eastern Parkway happening that attracts more than one and a half million people each year. Here, almost lost in the crowd, are sound trucks providing a Caribbean beat for both the crowd and costumed parade participants. (Kenwin Lezama Jr.)

Five

ACCIDENTS
AND INCIDENTS

Given its centuries-long span as a rural farming community, new homestead for benevolent institutions, upscale location for the moneyed and influential, and boomtown for real estate developers, both mundane and noteworthy events have shaped Crown Heights' development and name recognition.

Early newspaper reports, dating back to at least the 1850s, provide the researcher with an excellent overview of the community's past, including its hunting accidents, squatter evictions, horse thefts, devastating fires, and joyous celebrations. For the most part, central Brooklyn, and the neighborhood that became known as Crown Heights, lacked the larger name recognition common to its bordering neighbors of Flatbush and Bedford.

But that anonymity changed on August 19, 1991, when racially charged riots drew the attention of the world and made Crown Heights a household name. Tragedy and loss of life have always dominated the media, and this unfortunate neighborhood incident proved to be no exception.

The intricate details of the traffic death of a seven-year-old Guyanese black boy, the stabbing and death of a Australian rabbinical student, and the ensuing three-day riot can be found in almost every major newspapers across the county and dealt with more comprehensively than possible in this limited space.

In the end, lack of communication and the impact of cultural differences were found to be the sparks that set off the conflict, which Seton Hall University professor Edward Shapiro called, "The only anti-Semitic riot to take place in America."

Years of mediation, ecumenical discussions, and a sincere desire to exist peacefully with mutual respect ultimately combined to create the multicultural, multiracial community seen today. Over time, the neighborhood has grown and prospered, with an influx of new community residents, largely from Manhattan and the tristate area, purchasing homes, creating businesses, and adding new elements to the local demographic.

Only the passage of time will diminish the neighborhood stigma associated with the 1991 tragedy, but the peace and progress enjoyed in the last 18 years are sound evidence that the efforts appear to be working.

A boy, whose name could not be ascertained, had his left hand badly fractured yesterday, in the vicinity of Franklin-avenue and the Clove Road, Brooklyn, while hunting, by the accidental discharge of a gun in the hands of a companion.

A Moral City.

At the opening of the present term of the Brooklyn City Court there was no Grand Jury organized, because the District-Attorney stated to the Court that there was little or no work for them to do. Brooklyn has a population in the vicinity of 200,000 souls.

☞ Brooklyn City Court Calendar for Monday next: Nos. 3, 4, 5, 7, 8, 8½, 10, 11, 12, 13, 15, 16, 23, 25, 26, 27, 28, 29, 30, 31.

The rural nature that was once Crown Heights is detailed here by the report of a boy who had his left hand badly fractured while hunting at Franklin Avenue and Clove Road when a friend's rifle accidentally discharged. Brooklyn had a population of only 200,000 at the time, and it was evidently peaceful because no Brooklyn Grand Jury was organized due to lack of work. (Brooklyn Daily Eagle.)

This painting by Philadelphia-native Charles Lewis Fussell (1840–1909) captures the ire of a shanty inhabitant on Crow Hill in the 1890s during his visit to late-19th-century Brooklyn. The Pennsylvania Academy of the Fine Arts owns six of Fussell's Crow Hill paintings, including a barren landscape on a ridge depicting wood frame houses and the Crow Hill penitentiary, the image's most identifiable feature. (Schwarz Gallery, Philadelphia.)

Guilty of murdering two and the attempted murder of his girlfriend and brother, convicted felon Alexander Jefferson made news around the country in the 1880s. Known as the Crow Hill Murders, documented ongoing appeals to reverse the death sentence (which reached New York governor Grover Cleveland's desk) provide an overview of the poverty, lifestyle, topography, and brutality of the times. Jefferson was ineptly executed on August 1, 1884, in a prolonged hanging at the Raymond Street Jail. His brain was later removed for pathological study. (New York Times.)

THE CROW HILL TRAGEDY.

ALEXANDER JEFFERSON, THE COLORED MURDERER, ON TRIAL.

The trial of Alexander Jefferson for the murder of Emma Jackson and Henry Hicks, at Crow Hill, on the 21st of December last was begun in the Kings County Court of Sessions, before Judge Moore, yesterday. All parties were colored. About two hours were spent in getting a jury, after which Assistant District Attorney Backus opened the case for the prosecution. On the night of the murder Emma Jackson, an old colored woman, Henry Hicks, a colored boarder of Mrs. Jackson's, the latter's daughter, Annie Jackson, and Celestial Jefferson, a brother of the murderer, were sitting in Mrs. Jackson's cabin on Crow Hill, near the Kings County Penitentiary. Alexander Jefferson, armed with a double-bareled shot-gun, went to the window of the cabin, and, taking aim, shot his brother in the side of the head. He then fired another shot, which instantly killed Henry Hicks. Celestial Jefferson, after he was shot ran out of the shanty, and met Alexander on the threshold of the door coming in. A struggle ensued between the brothers, and Celestial obtained possession of the gun, with which he ran to the Twelfth Precinct Station-house to inform the Police of the murder. Alexander meantime entered the shanty, and, drawing a knife from his pocket, cut Mrs. Jackson's throat. He also stabbed her several times. He next attacked the young woman, Annie Jackson, and stabbed her in nine places. Jefferson, supposing he had murdered both of the women, then fled. When the Police arrived they found Mrs. Jackson's dead body at the foot of the hill upon which the shanty stood. The young woman, Annie Jackson, although badly wounded, recovered, as did also Celestial Jefferson. Several days after the murder Alexander Jefferson was found concealed under the floor of a disused factory not a quarter of a mile from the scene of the tragedy. When he saw that arrest was inevitable

Linda Gilbert (1847–1895), a noted prison reformer dedicated to the humane treatment of inmates in the 1800s, paid daily visits to prisoner Alexander Jefferson in his Brooklyn cell. Her *Sketch of the Life and Work of Linda Gilbert*, printed in 1876, details her efforts to obtain prison libraries resulting in the creation of the Gilbert Library and Prisoners' Aid Fund. (Public domain.)

Ota Benga, a 23-year-old Batwan from what was once the African Belgian Congo, was brought to the United States by missionary Samuel P. Verner, who was contracted to bring back pygmies for a St. Louis World's Fair exhibition. Months later, Benga traveled with Verner to the Bronx Zoo where, through a series of events, he was encouraged to hang a hammock and live in the Monkey House as part of a lucrative exhibit. (Public domain.)

COLORED ORPHAN HOME GETS THE PIGMY

He Has a Room to Himself and May Smoke If He Likes.

TO BE EDUCATED IF POSSIBLE

When He Returns to the Congo He May Then Help to Civilize His People.

Ota Benga has left the New York Zoological Park, in the Bronx, and has been installed in the Howard Colored Orphan Asylum, Dean Street and Troy Avenue, Brooklyn. There it is hoped that by association with the colored children and their instructors the pigmy may be civilized, so that when he goes back home he will be able to teach his people.

The teachers in the orphan asylum realize that they have a difficult problem, but they are hopeful of Ota Benga. He is in an institution where the inmates are children. Not larger than they, he

Upon learning of this arrangement, local black ministers demanded Benga be removed from the monkey cage and taken under the guardianship of J. H. Gordon, director of the church-sponsored Howard Colored Orphan Asylum in Weeksville. In January 1910, Gordon arranged to relocate Benga to Lynchburg, Virginia. (Brooklyn Daily Eagle.)

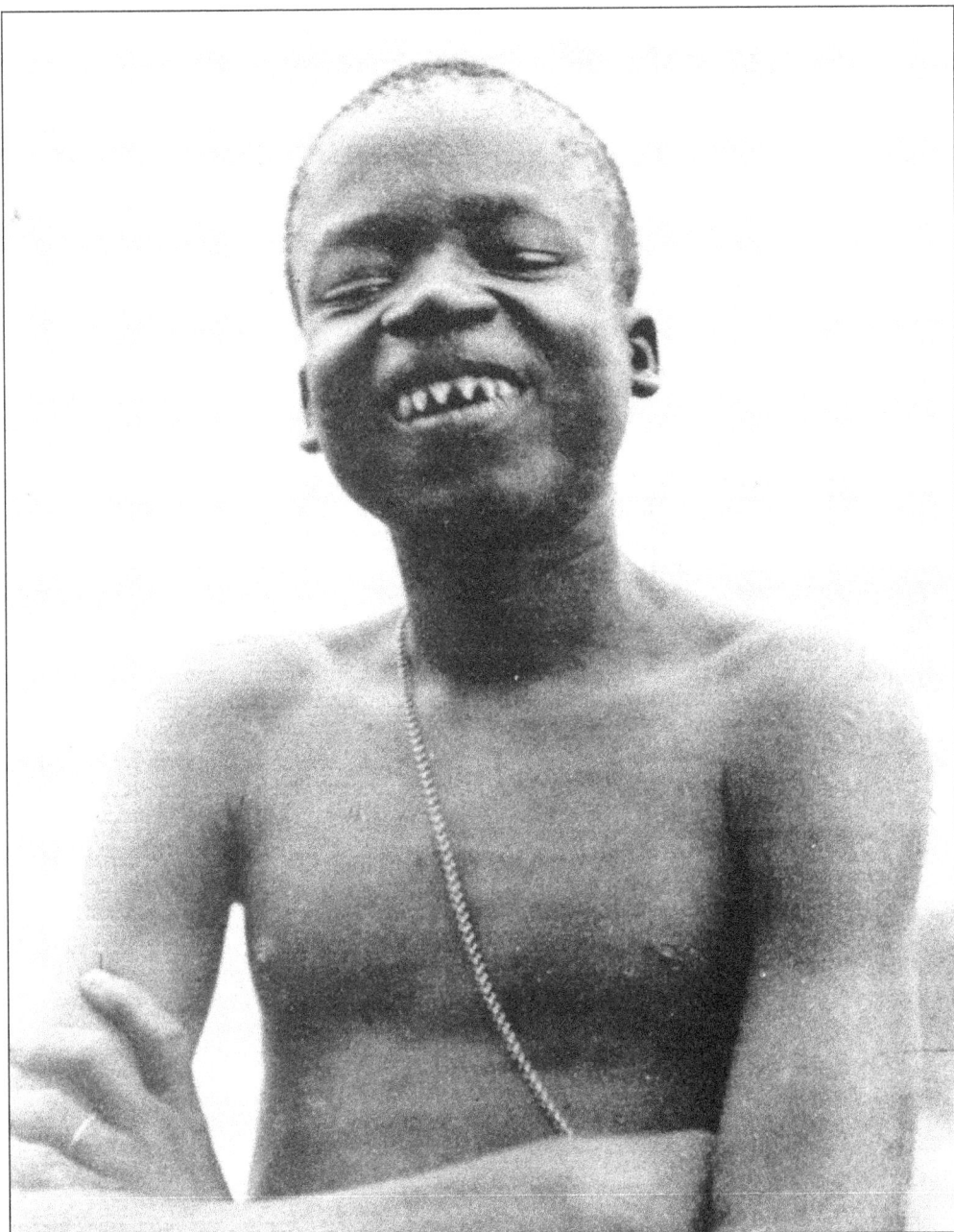

While in Virginia, Benga's teeth were capped, and he briefly attended classes at the Virginia Theological Seminary and College. Although dressed in American-style clothing, he reportedly preferred to roam the nearby woods with his bow and arrow. Taking a job at the local tobacco factory, he was a valuable employee because of his ability to reach tobacco leaves without using ladders. Over the years, Benga became depressed as he realized he could never return to Africa and that he was viewed consistently as a curiosity. Ultimately, on March 20, 1916, he built a ceremonial fire, chipped the caps off his teeth, and shot himself in the heart with a pistol he managed to secure. Oral reports indicate Ota Benga is buried in local White Rock Cemetery. (Public domain.)

" Aunt Abbie " Dead at 113 Years.

Mrs. Abbie Bingham, or '" Aunt Abbie," as she was also known in the neighborhood, a negress, who, her relatives and friends assert, was 113 years old, died at her home, 186 Buffalo Avenue, Brooklyn, on Friday. She lived with her youngest daughter, Mrs. Emma Etfell, who is 55 years of age. She leaves another daughter, who is said to be 75 years old, and a son who is 58 years old. Mrs. Etfell said yesterday that her mother was born in Norfolk, Va., in 1797.

The population of Weeksville was comprised primarily of African Americans who resided locally or traveled north for better education and job opportunities. Abbie Bingham, who lived at 186 Buffalo Avenue (off Bergen Street), was born in Norfolk, Virginia, in 1797, made her home in Weeksville, and reportedly lived to see the passage of 113 years. "Aunt Abbie" was survived by a daughter of 75 years of age, a son of 58, and another daughter of 55 at her death in 1910. (New York Times.)

The rural nature of this intersection of Dean Street at Buffalo Avenue in the early 1900s would be consistent with the essence of the Weeksville neighborhood Abbie Bingham knew during her many years living in the area. The buildings, as well as the barely discernable Hebrew Orphanage (peaked building silhouetted in the center of the photograph), have all been torn town and replaced by the high-rise Kingsborough houses. (New York Public Library.)

In 1869, the Society of the City of Brooklyn (founded in 1833) purchased 47 lots at Kingston and Atlantic Avenues for $31,000 to build new housing for the orphanage. Sitting on the Crown Heights/Bedford-Stuyvesant border of Atlantic Avenue, the structure was completed in June 1872, and 135 children moved in. By 1882, 367 children lived in the facility. (Brian Merlis.)

A fire consumed the building of the Orphan Asylum of the City of Brooklyn in the 1950s, resulting in the near-total destruction of the structure. Here only the steepled peak is recognizable as firemen train their hoses on the facility. The one-block area is now St. Andrew's Park. (Brooklyn Public Library Brooklyn Collection.)

Set in an obviously undeveloped section of Brooklyn, at the corner of Albany Avenue and Troy Avenue, the Roman Catholic St. John's Home orphan asylum society for boys was one of the leading charitable institutions in the borough. The institution was founded in 1829, with a location at 188 Jay Street. They removed to Willoughby and Bedford Avenues in 1858 and then occupied this building in 1870 after two years of construction. (New York City Municipal Archives.)

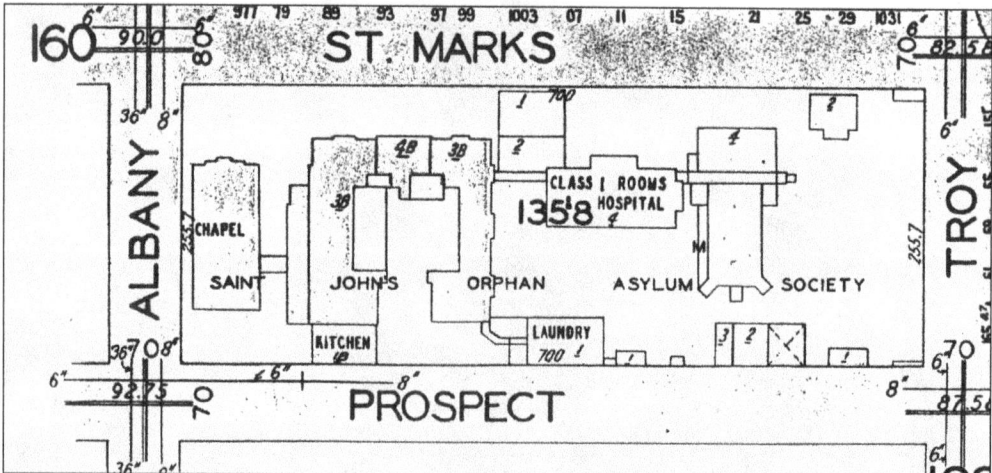

The square block occupation of the St. John's Orphan Asylum Society indicated at the above grid included a chapel, kitchen, hospital room, and laundry. Today the Albany Housing Projects have replaced the institution, which burned to the ground in 1884. (New York City Municipal Archives.)

The magnificent architecture of the once grand St. John's Home for orphaned boys is evident, even given the grainy-effects of this years-old image. With a frontage of 170 feet and depth of 210 feet, it was built of freestone, three stories in height, and crowned by a high mansard roof. With construction completed in 1870, the cost of the building exceeded $200,000. A fire on December 19, 1884, resulted in the loss of 36-year-old Sister Mary Josephine, who became trapped on the mansard roof, slipped and fell to her death in attempting to gain access to a fireman's rescue ladder. She expired at nearby St. Mary's Hospital. (Brooklyn Public Library Brooklyn Collection.)

Recognized as the worst mass transit accident in United States history, the Malbone Street wreck of November 1918 occurred on a hairpin turn at the entrance to a tunnel located just beneath Prospect Park and nearby Ebbets Field. Some 93 people lost their lives, with many decapitated and others electrocuted when the power was at first turned off immediately following the accident and then turned on again prematurely. As in a "perfect storm," the circumstance of a transit strike by the Brotherhood of Locomotive Engineers (LBE), a train driven by inexperienced motorman Edward Luciano, a steep downward incline on the approach to the tunnel, and the flimsy wooden construction of the individual cars, all combined to create the devastation suffered on November 1, 1918. As a result of the tragic name association, Malbone Street was renamed to Empire Boulevard, a name it still carries today. (Public domain.)

Standing shoulder-to-shoulder outside the East New York Savings Bank on the corner of Utica Avenue and Eastern Parkway in the 1930s, men and one woman, left, crowd the sidewalk in anticipation of gaining access to the bank and their money. This run on the bank was repeated around the country at the start of the Great Depression, a financial condition that endured until the start of World War II. (New York Public Library.)

The lighting fixtures are gone, but the bank with its recognizable clock face and glass-paned entrance can still be found on the same Crown Heights corner in 2009. No longer East New York Savings Bank, it sits next door to the Roman Catholic St. Matthew's Church, a longtime resident of the neighborhood.

The 1991 Crown Heights riots that erupted with the deaths of a seven-year-old Guyanese boy and an Australian rabbinical student occurred 18 years ago, an event that largely dominated the tenure of Mayor David Dinkins and Police Commissioner Lee Brown. Since that time, mayors Dinkins (1990–1993), Rudolph Giuliani (1994–2001), and Michael Bloomberg (2002–), above, have all worked with noteworthy success to keep community and municipal lines of communication open. (New York Public Library.)

New York City councilman and ex-police officer James E. Davis (1962–2003) was shot and killed inside Manhattan's city hall on June 23 by a political rival he had escorted past the building's metal detectors. A Crown Heights resident who lived on Brooklyn Avenue near Eastern Parkway, Davis founded a not-for-profit organization in 1990 dedicated to stopping violence in American cities.

Outside the home of Thelma Davis on Brooklyn Avenue, the mission of her son councilman James Davis is not forgotten. The four-story building displays an ever-present American flag and a banner reading "One Community, Stop the Violence." The work of this not-for-profit organization founded by James is being continued by his brother Jeffrey.

NASA astronaut Ronald McNair (left) was killed during the launch of the space shuttle *Challenger* on January 28, 1986, along with Michael Smith, Dick Scobee, Elison Onizuka, teacher Christa McAuliffe, Gregory Jarvis, and Judith Resnik. Here McNair poses with Col. Guion S. Bluford (center) and Col. Frederick D. Gregory in 1985 as they await mission assignments.

A native of South Carolina, with a physics doctorate from the Massachusetts Institute of Technology, 36-year-old Dr. McNair was memorialized in Brooklyn's Crown Heights with the 1994 unveiling of a 1.36-acre, triangle-shaped park bordered by Eastern Parkway and Washington and Classon Avenues. McNair's profile can be discerned here on the nine-foot, pyramid-shaped monument of polished red granite.

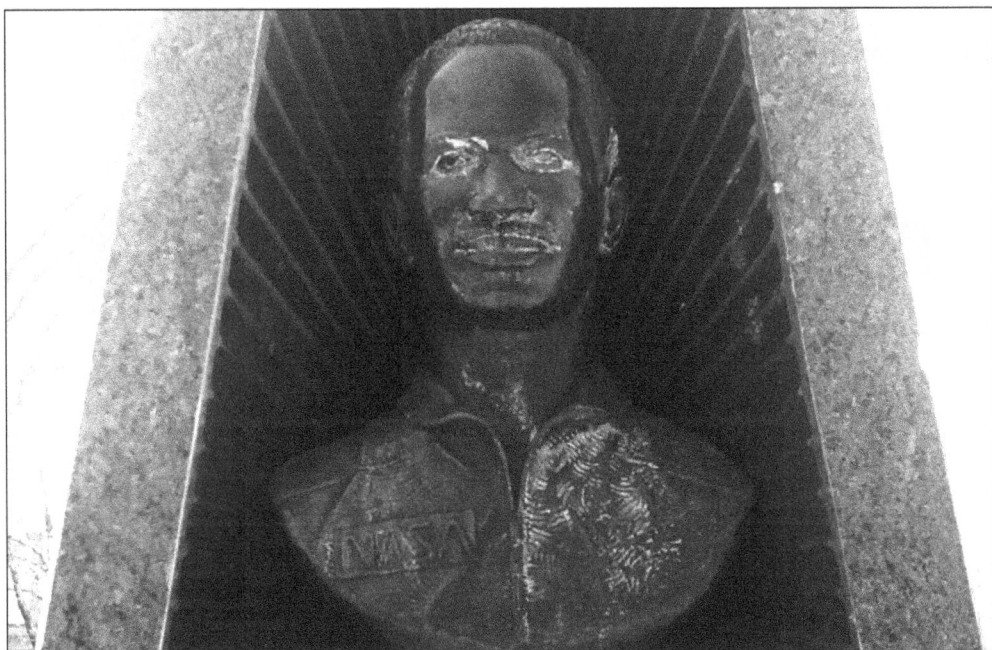

The bronze portrait of Dr. McNair is the work of sculpture artist Ogundipe Fayomi. This granite and bronze memorial, recognizing the brilliant mind and accomplishments of McNair, is a daily reminder of personal and academic excellence for local students attending the three schools on three consecutive blocks that face the McNair Park, which are Prospect Heights High School, Clara Barton High School, and the LaSalle School for the Deaf.

Curtis Mayfield (1942–1999) was a remarkable musical talent who enjoyed early stardom starting in the 1960s. A composer of inspiring civil rights era anthems, his sound track to the 1972 film *Superfly*, brought wide recognition of his musical genius. Mayfield became a paraplegic when a freakish, but short-lived gust of wind toppled sound equipment at a 1994 performance at Wingate athletic field. Just outside the Crown Heights border, Wingate is the neighborhood's local high school. (Public domain.)

The New York Urban League Brooklyn branch resided for decades in this red-stone building at 1251 Dean Street, servicing the housing, educational, social, and employment needs of people of color who moved to the north in great numbers in the early 20th century. The organization was founded in 1906 by Frances A. Kelor as the National League for the Protection of Colored Women and merged in 1911 with two other organizations (Committee for Improving the Industrial Condition of Negroes in New York and Committee on Urban Conditions Among Negroes) to form the National League on Urban Conditions Among Negroes, shortened to the National Urban League. The Dean Street office closed in 2002.

Six

ARCHITECTURAL GEMS

Like many of America's urban townships and neighborhoods, Crown Heights and Weeksville have a deep, centuries-long history. It is unfortunate that much is all but forgotten by the local community, including the municipal schools that teach that history.

Remarkably, however, a few traces of urban design and expansion still remain, often explaining why a road ends abruptly or runs a certain way, why a parcel of land stands in isolation along a busy thoroughfare, or why one section of town is endowed with newer buildings or more ornate architecture than another.

Because demolition, rather than preservation, has often been the rule in New York City's growth, too many buildings have been kicked over in the name of progress or allowed to deteriorate through neglect. Ironically the most decrepit-looking building has the deepest history, a quality that makes the structure even more worthy of rescue.

Fortunately Crown Heights, and the smaller township of Weeksville within it, has had a number of champions who stepped forward to protect that unique history. Most notably, Joan Maynard of the Weeksville Society and Jim Hurley of the Long Island Historical Society challenged the demolition of several frame houses in the heart of Brooklyn, which were once a part of a vibrant African American community and almost completely forgotten. Today those buildings represent the Weeksville Heritage Center, formerly known as the Society for the Preservation of Weeksville and Bed-Stuyvesant History, with construction of a museum and cultural center scheduled to take place.

Selected blocks in the north of Crown Heights received historic designation in 2006 to protect the remarkable architecture, free-standing mansions, and vintage frame houses that dot the community and comprise its unique character. Many have been lost over the decades, most notably along St. Mark's Avenue, where an entire two-block stretch of vintage structures once stood. Now only photographs capture their vanished grandeur.

Overbuilding continues to present a threat to the neighborhood, with block-deep, multistory buildings towering over two-story homes, not only affecting the circulation and quality of air, but also aggravating an already dense population. Vigilance and united community effort is required to protect and enhance the architectural beauty of the neighborhood shown on the following pages.

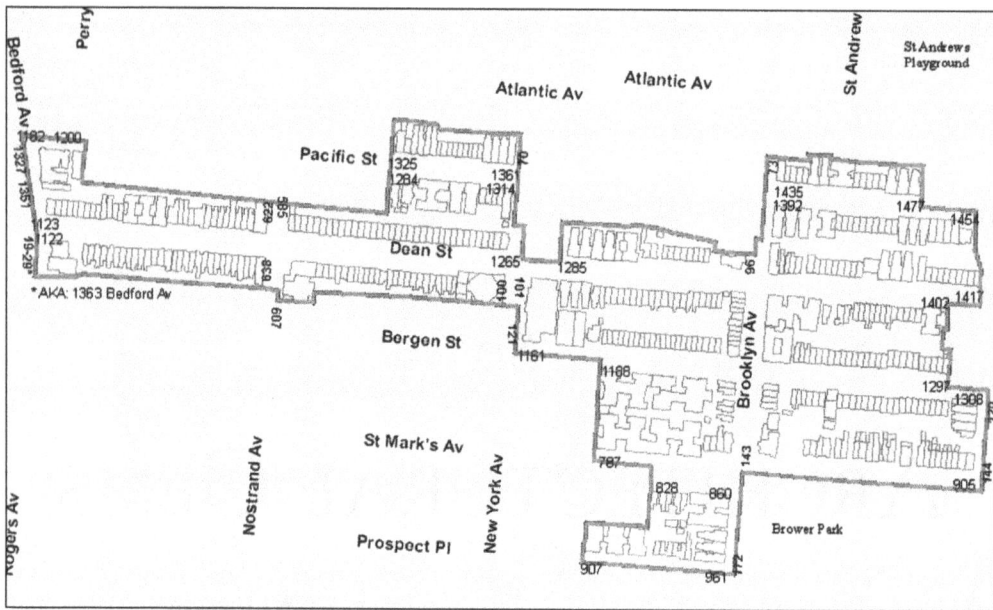

In April 2007, the New York City Landmarks Preservation Commission (LPC) voted unanimously to grant landmark protection to 472 buildings in the Crown Heights North section of Brooklyn. The above map details the district boundary lines that delineate vintage buildings constructed between the 1850 and 1930s.

The bell roof of this pair of 1892 houses is a distinguishing feature that marks its identity in the vintage photograph of the Brooklyn Children's Museum mansion home seen on page 90. The buildings at 855 and 857 St. Mark's Avenue are now protected from demolition by landmark designation acquired in 2007. Representing the finest in Romanesque Revival–style architecture, the buildings were designed by Montrose Morris, an acclaimed late-19th-century architect.

Established on Bergen Street off Rogers Avenue as the Bedford Heights Baptist Church, and constructed in 1888, this ivy-covered edifice still stands today, although its brownstone brickwork is now abutted by adjoining structures. Today the Ebenezer Wesleyan Methodist Church resides here and has since 1939.

The Evangelical Lutheran Church of the Epiphany at 721 Lincoln Place was founded in 1907 in what was then considered the Bedford section of Brooklyn. Primarily comprised of an English-speaking German congregation and led by first pastor Rev. W. H. Stutts, D.D., the church built its first edifice on Sterling Place. It was replaced by this remarkable structure, designed in early English Gothic style, on the adjoining lot fronting Lincoln Place in 1925.

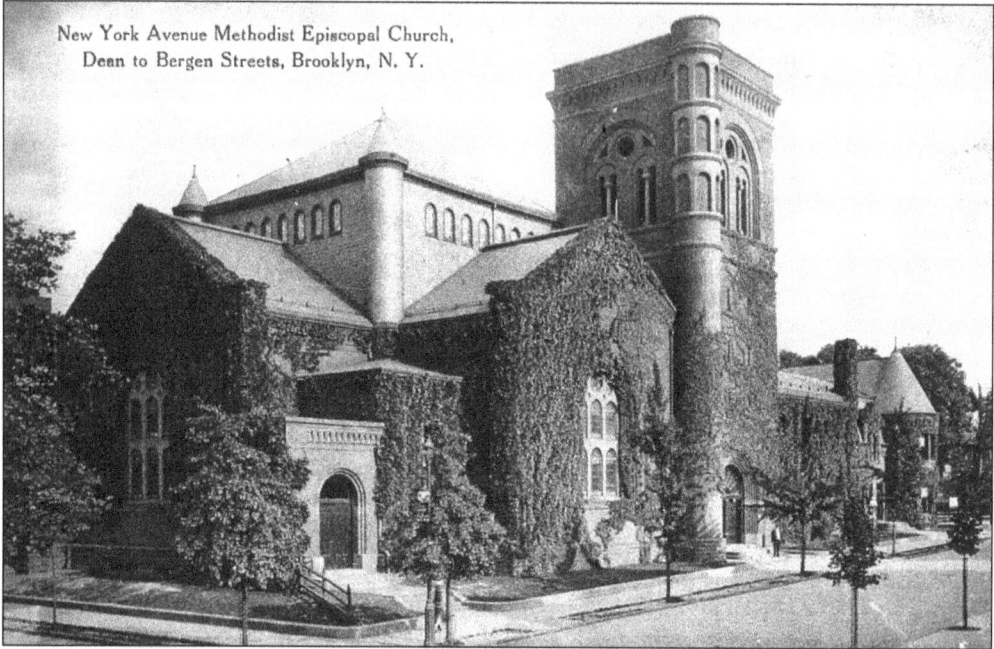

New York Avenue Methodist Episcopal Church,
Dean to Bergen Streets, Brooklyn, N. Y.

The New York Avenue Methodist Episcopal Church building, which includes a school and parsonage, was designed by architect J. C. Cady and built in 1892 as a beautiful example of Romanesque Revival design. Considered to be among the largest and most influential churches of this denomination of its time, the church society built and managed the Methodist Episcopal Home for Aged Men on nearby Park Place and New York Avenue, which still stands today.

Union United Methodist Church assumed ownership of the edifice in 1948 and continued to maintain the integrity of the building exterior even before it fell under landmark guidelines. Located at 101 New York Avenue or 1270–1276 Dean Street, the building took four years (1889–1892) to complete.

This freestanding three-story masonry house, known as the Old Heintz Mansion, was still at the corner of Bergen Street and New York Avenue in 1923. The steeple of the Methodist Episcopal Church, located at New York Avenue and Dean Street, can be seen in the rear. Very little else in the near vicinity of the huge lot can be seen. (Brooklyn Public Library Brooklyn Collection.)

The Dean Sage House at 839 St. Mark's Avenue is considered to be among the oldest and most important mansions remaining in Crown Heights North. Sage, who was a wealthy lumber dealer, commissioned architect Russell Sturgis to build this High Victorian Gothic structure, since Sturgis was considered to be that era's finest practitioner in this style. Today it is one of the rarest and finest examples of Sturgis's work in New York City.

Reportedly constructed in anticipation of the 1883 opening of the Brooklyn Bridge, this 1882 Italianate, neo-Greco house is one of the few surviving freestanding houses in Crown Heights North. Designed by George Damen and considered to be exceptionally well preserved, the one-family structure at 1450–1452 Pacific Street was converted to a two-family house by 1931.

Individually designated as a New York City landmark in 1997, this freestanding Queen Anne home of red brick, sandstone, and granite trim was designed by the Parfitt Brothers in 1887. A number of prominent families have resided in the home, including stove manufacturer John Truslow; Rev. Adolphus J. F. Behrends of the Central Congregational Church; Maria de Angel, wife of coffee exporter Alezandro de Angel; and Dr. Ethlin Lamos, who lived in the property at 1331 Dean Street from 1943 to 1995.

This freestanding mansion located on St. Mark's Avenue fell victim to ceaseless demolition and overdevelopment during an era when preservation was not a priority. The Eiler mansion was a large wood frame house with cupola located at 751 St. Mark's Avenue. A signed notice, dated April 21, 1935, informs the public that it is, "To be town down to put up apartments," most likely matching those seen on New York and St. Mark's Avenues, shown below.

St. Mark's Avenue today is a cavernous row of six-story, half-timbered apartment buildings. It is difficult to imagine that Victorian mansions once lined this commodious double-wide street, which has been narrowed to provide additional parking space.

The Brooklyn Jewish Center on Eastern Parkway between Brooklyn and New York Avenues was founded in 1919, and the cornerstone was laid in 1920. It housed a sanctuary, day school, swimming pool, and health club under founding rabbi Israel H. Levinthal until 1954. Resident Abraham Beame (later mayor of New York City) was an active member. Today it is a Talmudical Seminary.

The synagogue on Eastern Parkway north, near Albany Avenue, is the Israel Henry Beren Torah Center and United Lubavitch Yesheva. Constructed of brick and limestone, it sits on a high base and is accented by Ionic columns. The institute's residency hall is also nearby on President Street between Kingston and Albany Avenues.

Wealthy merchant James B. Laing purchased this 17-room Queen Anne–style home in 1898. Designed by Henry B. Hill and built by Jordan L. Snedecor, this semiattached mansion at 118–120 Brooklyn Avenue at Bergen Street is one of the few to have survived successive eras of aggressive demolition.

Constructed in the arts and crafts style of white stucco with grey slate roofs, these houses at 935–947 Prospect Place, built between 1920 and 1922, have shared chimneys and driveways with garages in the rear yards. Designed by A. White Pierce, the quaint one-and-a-half-story homes are the only style of the kind in the landmark district.

Once known as Doctor's Row, the still impressive mansions that stand on President Street between Kingston and New York Avenues are reminiscent of the homes that used to line St. Mark's Avenue between 1900 and into the 1920s. Clergymen, doctors, dentists, and a number of institutions live on these blocks in Crown Heights South today.

This current photograph of Grant Square provides in a single image three of the most identifiable landmarks at the Crown Heights/Bedford-Stuyvesant border of Bedford Avenue near Atlantic Avenue. Here the definitive Gen. Ulysses S. Grant statue, facing north on Bedford Avenue, the former Swedish Hospital, and the crenelated 23rd Regiment Armory share the same frame, removing all doubt that one is indeed viewing a photograph of Central Brooklyn.

This elementary school, PS 138 at Park Place between Nostrand and Rogers Avenues, demonstrates the time, care, and masonry skills that were devoted to New York Public Schools in the early years of municipal construction. This four-story brick building acknowledges the city's Dutch and Native American history with a stone-carved seal of the City of New York placed to the right of the building entrance. In clear and intricate detail, a Dutchman and Native American in native garb flank a windmill-embossed shield upon which an American bald eagle is perched.

St. Bartholomew's Anglican Church on Pacific Street near Bedford Avenue received individual landmark designation years before Crown Heights North was recognized for historic preservation. Looking very much like an old English country parish, its history includes the church memberships of many distinguished families of Colonial descent. Its beauty is also enhanced by priceless stained-glass windows that must be seen to be appreciated.

In stark contrast, this forlorn two-story structure, with pitched roof and wood-lathe siding, is boarded up and awaiting demolition. Located at 1531 Dean Street near Schenectady Avenue in Weeksville, it is only a matter of time before the building and its history are removed and forgotten.

BIBLIOGRAPHY

An Introduction to the Black Contribution to the Development of Brooklyn. Brooklyn, NY: New Muse Community Museum of Brooklyn, 1977.

Brooklyn Daily Eagle, "St. John's Day in Pigtown: Italian Colony Celebrating the Festival in Splendid Style," June 24, 1902.

Brooklyn Daily Eagle, "Strolls Upon Old Lines: Crow Hill and Some of Its Suggestions," December 9, 1888.

Brooklyn Daily Eagle, "Traces of Clove Road: An Historic Highway Now Almost Effaced," July 31, 1887.

Burns, Peter. *Curtis Mayfield.* London: Sanctuary Publishing, 2003.

Caratas, Michael D., and Cynthia Danza. *Crown Heights North Historic District Designation Report.* New York: New York City Landmarks Preservation Commission, 2007.

Cudahy, Brian. *The Malbone Street Wreck.* New York: Fordham University Press, 1999.

Gilbert, Linda. *The Life and Work of Linda Gilbert.* New York: Industrial School of the Hebrew Orphan Asylum, 1876.

Livingstone, John H. *The Citizen's Guide to Brooklyn and Long Island.* Jersey City, NJ: Jersey City Printing Company, 1893.

Manders, Eric I. *The Battle of Long Island.* Monmouth Beach, NJ: Philip Freneau Press, 1978.

Maynard, Joan, and Gwen Cottman. *Weeksville, Then and Now.* Brooklyn, NY: Society for the Preservation of Weeksville and Bedford-Stuyvesant History, 1983.

Morrone, Francis. *An Architectural Guidebook to Brooklyn.* Layton, UT: Gibbs Smith, 2001.

New York Times, "Evicting Squatters is Not an Easy Task," November 20, 1910.

Shapiro, Edward S. *Crown Heights: Blacks, Jews, and the 1991 Brooklyn Riot.* Lebanon, NH: University Press of New England, 2006.

Taylor, Clarence. *The Black Churches of Brooklyn.* New York: Columbia University Press, 1994.

Visit us at
arcadiapublishing.com

www.ingramcontent.com/pod-product-compliance
Lightning Source LLC
Chambersburg PA
CBHW080616110426
42813CB00006B/1528